R. Haveman

THE
ECONOMICS
OF THE
RICH

D0733986

THE ECONOMICS OF THE RICH

HOWARD P. TUCKMAN
Florida State University

🏠 RANDOM HOUSE
New York

First Edition
987654321
Copyright © 1973 by Random House, Inc.

All rights reserved under International and
Pan-American Copyright Conventions. No part
of this book may be reproduced in any form
or by any means, electronic or mechanical,
including photocopying, without permission
in writing from the publisher. All inquiries
should be addressed to Random House, Inc.,
201 East 50th Street, New York, N.Y. 10022.
Published in the United States by Random
House, Inc., and simultaneously in Canada by
Random House of Canada Limited, Toronto.

Library of Congress Cataloging in Publication Data

Tuckman, Howard P
    The Economics of the Rich.
Includes bibliographical references.
1. Wealth—United States. 2. Income—United
States. I. Title.
HC 110.W4T8   330.1'6   73-12990
ISBN 0-394-31714-9

Manufactured in the United States of America

Design by Gloria Gentile

To Barbara—
my wife,
adviser, and colleague

ACKNOWLEDGMENTS

I would like to express my thanks to the friends and colleagues who offered me their advice and assistance. Professor E. Ray Canterbery read most of the chapters in the original manuscript. His lively wit and irreverent observations were a constant source of inspiration. Professors Robert Lekachman, Stephen Michelson, Raymond Franklin, and Robert Lampman also enlivened the text with their helpful criticisms and stimulating suggestions. I am especially grateful to my wife Barbara and my research assistant Gary Brosch for reading several drafts of this book and continually reminding me of the virtues of clarity and directness. The suggestions of Professors E. Lester Levine and Robert Mitchell are also acknowledged. Two students, Mike Sobel and Kathy Adams, also commented on the manuscript. Special thanks are due to the secretarial staff of the Institute of Social Research for their technical assistance and to Dr. Charles Grigg, director of the institute, for his encouragement. Mrs. Jeannette Buckley did an able job of typing the final draft. Barbara Conover, Edward Cone, and Paul Shensa of the Random House editorial staff also helped greatly to expedite the publication of this book.

I would also like to express my gratitude to *The New York Times* for permission to reprint excerpts from Russell Baker's "The Secret Weapon of Daddy Warbucks" and to CBS News for providing access to information on the negotiations for the sale of U.S. wheat to the Soviet Union during the summer of 1972.

CONTENTS

THE
ECONOMICS
OF THE
RICH

INTRODUCTION

We read about affluent America in magazines and books, and we see it celebrated on television and in the movies. We are also increasingly aware of another America, a never-never land of the unskilled, including blacks, whites, and Mexican-Americans, of teenage and aged dropouts, of families headed by women unable to enter the labor force, and of thousands upon thousands of hungry children. John Kenneth Galbraith's *The Affluent Society*, Michael Harrington's *The Other America*, and many other books, papers, and congressional hearings, some of epic proportions, remind us that poverty has not been eliminated.

But there is a third and largely forgotten America, one that has slipped from view to be replaced by the vociferously fought, and only partially won, war on poverty. This is the America of property and privilege, the land of the wealthy. Although statistics on wealth are not kept on a systematic basis in the United States, there are several indications that the distribution of income has remained stagnant despite our growing affluence. While incomes clearly became more nearly equal during the Depression and World War II, the distribution of income has barely changed since.

The rich are nearly as "invisible" as the poor were during the Eisenhower years. In 1963 Harrington wrote: "The millions who are poor in the United States tend to become increasingly invisible. Here is a great mass of people, yet it takes an effort of the intellect and will to see them." At about the same time that Harrington was setting his pen to paper, the Federal Reserve Board estimated the number of millionaires to be more than 80,000, and it found over 4 million households with incomes greater than $50,000. The members of many of these households lived a quiet and luxurious life in private communities tucked far away from the prying eyes of the public.

Pockets of wealth still exist throughout the United States. Pikeville, Kentucky, is an example. Conventional wisdom holds that everyone in Appalachia qualifies as a prime candidate for the welfare rolls. Nonetheless, the *St. Petersburg Times* reported that Pikeville, a town of 4,700, represents a veritable showcase of wealth! According to local bankers, the area has more than 50 millionaires and claims 25 doctors, 35 lawyers, a Cadillac dealership with a waiting list, and a 7-million-dollar hospital under construction. Most of this wealth is a result of the recent coal boom that has brought prosperity to parts of eastern Kentucky. Apparently, everything that the residents of the coal town touch seems to turn to gold. Yet recent Census Bureau figures show that more than half of the people in surrounding Pike County had gross incomes below the 1969 federal poverty line of $3,700 for a family of four.

In order to understand why a rising level of affluence does not lead to greater income equality in the United States, we shall seek answers to a series of questions. How many people accumulate wealth in large amounts? Who are the wealthy? Do today's rich maintain the special privileges enjoyed by their counterparts at the turn of the century? Does government policy aid or abet their goals? Will the less affluent members of our society catch up with the favored minority as incomes continue to rise and as more people obtain a higher education? Is the accumulation of wealth good or bad? Should our tax and expenditure policies be changed? If so, in what ways? The answers to these questions provide fascinating reading. And they raise several potent questions regarding the direction of our economic and social policies.

It is our thesis that both the economic system and its laws and institutions favor people with large incomes. To support this thesis, we shall identify and explore the various sources of income. Chapter 1 provides a brief discussion of these sources. Chapter 2 then considers the difficulties in determining who the affluent really are, and it provides a profile of the residents of the various way stations along the road to wealth. Its approach is somewhat unconventional in that we identify the wealthy in terms of their incomes rather than their assets. In common parlance, a person with a large savings account and substantial holdings of stocks, bonds, and real estate is said to be wealthy. A person with no assets and $50,000 of income is usually not considered to be wealthy. But both individuals enjoy a special place in our economic system and both have strong incentives to preserve the status quo. Thus both are of interest to us in this book. Since those with large assets usually also have high incomes, we shall use an income rather than an asset definition of wealth.

Having disposed of the problem of identifying the various stages of affluence, we shall focus on the policies that help those who are wealthy to create new wealth for themselves. Chapter 3 explores the role of inheritance taxes. Chapters 4 and 5 illustrate the various ways in which the government supports the wealthy, both directly through cash payments and indirectly through policies favorable to people with high incomes. Chapters 6 and 7 deal with the fascinating and complex world of tax subsidies, while in Chapter 8 we consider the mystical workings of capital markets and how they operate to the benefit of the wealthy. Chapters 9 and 10 examine the role of the educational establishment, beginning with the cradle and ending with the university. Along the way we point out the special role of private schools for the rich and the characteristics of public schools that tend to reinforce wealth. Finally, Chapter 11 brings together the key points made throughout the book in a discussion of policies that can be undertaken to control the warriors for wealth.

The Economics of the Rich is intended for both the intelligent layman and the student in an introductory course in economics, political science, or sociology. It tries to counter the biases introduced by many economists in discussions of how income is determined in a market economy; it also attempts to make economics more relevant to the issues of the seventies. No matter what the reader's political views are, we hope the issues raised in this book will provide an important insight into the processes by which wealth is accumulated.

1
ON THE
ORIGINS
OF WEALTH

*In the absence of statistical knowledge, it is
understandable that one should form an
impression of the American standard of living
from the full page magazine advertisements
portraying a jolly American family in an
air conditioned mansion, with a Mercedes,
a station wagon, a motor launch, and all the
other good things that go to make up
comfortable living. Actually, of course, this
sort of life is still beyond the grasp of
90 per cent of the American public and even
beyond most families from which the select
group of college students comes.*
—PAUL A. SAMUELSON

America is an affluent country. The Census Bureau estimates that median family income reached $9,800 in 1970 and that it will rise to $15,000—in 1970 dollars—by 1985. The share of personal income spent on things to use, touch, and enjoy—like automobiles, clothing, and recreation—has increased by 50 percent in the past quarter of a century. Never before has the average citizen commanded such a high standard of living or been able to spend his money on so wide a variety of goods. Economics textbooks proclaim the message for all to hear: "The king is dead, long live the consumer!"

Our rising level of affluence is misleading. It disguises the abject poverty at the bottom of our society, and it blurs our perception of the great opulence at the top. Often far away from the teeming suburbs of middle-class America live the fortunate recipients of a disproportionate share of the national income.

Only 5 percent of America's families receive 16 percent of the national income. Paul Samuelson portrays the situation more graphically: "If we made an income pyramid out of a child's blocks, with each layer portraying $1,000 of income, the peak would be far higher than the Eiffel Tower, but almost all of us would be within a yard of the ground."[1]

How do a few select families reach the income peak? Is this the natural outcome of a Darwinian "struggle for existence"? Are these the privileged members of the power elite, the military-industrial complex, or some vast worldwide conspiracy? We shall try to answer these questions in this chapter.

The distribution of income within a society is determined partially by the rules and institutions which that society chooses to adopt. The foundations of an economic system are established by a set of laws that determine both property ownership and the right of owners to deed their assets to others. Along with these rules come additional regulations governing barter and exchange—usually in support of the status quo distribution of resources. The operation of the economic system determines how national income is distributed and which goods and services are produced. The allocations of this system may then be sanctioned or modified by appropriate governmental policies.

These institutions and rules are complementary. The final distribution of income and wealth depends on the specific property rules adopted by a society. Similarly, social attitudes and governmental policies take shape in the context of a given distribution of income and within the framework of an economic system. Working in a circular fashion, social attitudes and policies, in turn, shape our property laws and other legal institutions. And these modify the distribution of income provided by the economic system.

Of course, this process is not a completely closed one. Social experiments, such as the "war on poverty" and public housing programs, reflect society's desire to interrupt the circular flow by introducing an element of equity into the system. Likewise, the progressive income tax represents an attempt to

[1] *Paul A. Samuelson, Economics, 9th ed. (New York: McGraw-Hill Book Company, 1973), p. 85.*

break the link between the marketplace and the final distribution of income. Unfortunately, however, the wealthy (people with high incomes) have learned to *internalize* the benefits of public programs. This makes it difficult to use public programs to break the circle.

The principle of *internalization* is an important one and will appear many times throughout this book. The government enacts a farm subsidy program, and the wealthy farmers benefit. It sells huge surpluses of wheat to the Soviet Union, and the large exporters reap the profits. It takes possession of slum housing, and the poor continue to be poorly housed, while a few landlords collect huge sums. We can observe this phenomenon at many different levels of government and in many different countries. Internalization is a common phenomenon wherever a pyramid type of income distribution exists. And such a distribution exists in most countries of the world today.

Because the rich are able to internalize the benefits of public programs, they find it worthwhile to try to influence public spending. Thus we find well-organized lobbying organizations designed to "protect" the expenditures of the Highway Trust Fund, to block cuts in farm subsidies, to ensure favorable treatment of income from the sale of stocks, and to protect wealthy investors against periodic assaults on their tax shelters. Internalization allows the wealthy to acquire more and more funds to protect their domain and to press for new programs and policies that will build the income pyramid even higher. Thus income and assets beget more income and assets, and the circle of wealth is once again closed.

In order to understand this process better, it will be useful to examine the sources of assets. By assets we shall mean holdings of money, stocks, bonds, real estate, and other forms of capital. As we shall see, those with the highest incomes in the United States also tend to have the largest assets. And it is our belief that those with high incomes should be labeled "the wealthy."

INCOME AND ASSETS

The greater one's income, the greater the money available to invest in income-producing assets, and the greater one's assets, the greater his income. People who begin with high incomes are in a better position to add to their fortunes than people with low incomes. The nouveaux riches find it difficult to rise very high in the income pyramid, while people who inherit old fortunes are comfortably ensconced at the peak. Ferdinand Lundberg, a well-known student of distribution processes, argues: "Nearly all the current large incomes, those exceeding $1 million, $500,000, or even $100,000 or $50,000 a year, are derived in fact from old property accumulations, by inheritors —that is, by people who never did whatever one is required to do, approved or disapproved, creative or noncreative, in order to assemble a fortune."[2]

Most American families accumulate assets out of income. This relationship holds whether we look at liquid assets alone (defined as savings and checking accounts, bonds, common stocks, and certificates of deposit) or at a measure that also includes real estate and other less liquid assets such as equity held in family-owned businesses. Figure 1 is based on information obtained from a 1962 survey conducted by the Federal Reserve Board.[3] The consumer units examined by the Federal Reserve consist of families and unrelated individuals. Subsequent, less thorough studies suggest that these data are still relevant. (In fact, it is a sad commentary on the state of the art that to the author's knowledge no subsequent studies have been conducted on so detailed a basis.)

Notice the dramatic patterns shown in Figure 1. Assets rise at an increasing rate as income rises, and the absolute amount of assets held in all categories rises with income.[4] The percentage of total assets held in the form of automobiles and liquid assets decreases as income increases; the percentage devoted to business and investment assets increases as income increases; and the percentage held in the form of housing first rises and then declines as income increases.

Most families acquire assets (and debts) in such a fashion

[2] *Ferdinand Lundberg*, The Rich and the Super Rich *(New York: Bantam Books, Inc., 1969), p. 155.*

[3] *Dorothy Projector and Gertrude Weiss*, Survey of Financial Characteristics of Consumers, *Federal Reserve Technical Papers, August 1966. Hereafter referred to as* Federal Reserve Survey.

[4] *The limits on asset accumulation are discussed in Chapter 11.*

Figure 1

COMPOSITION OF WEALTH HOLDINGS BY INCOME LEVEL

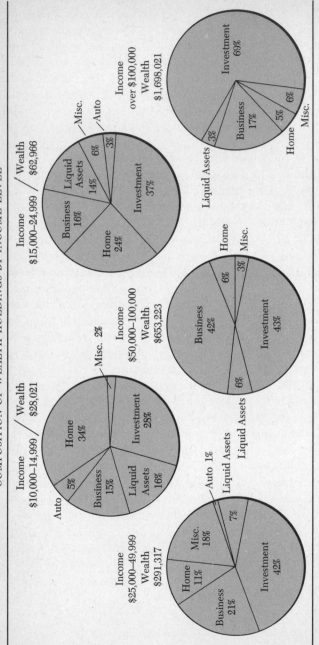

Source: Dorothy Projector and Gertrude Weiss, *Survey of Financial Characteristics of Consumers*, Federal Reserve Technical Papers, August 1966, p. 110.

as to balance their desire for income against their needs for liquidity and safety. The structure of a family's asset holdings depends on (1) its demand for the services of consumer durables, (2) its need for cash balances and liquid assets to provide for unexpected contingencies, (3) expected future expenditures (e.g., a child about to enter college, the need to set up a professional practice, etc.), (4) its ability to borrow and its information about—and attitudes toward—the capital market, (5) the occupational and other cash requirements of the family members, (6) the family's tax bracket, and (7) the difficulty (and costs) of making capital transactions.[5]

American families frequently own a home and an automobile. Many share their possessions with the finance company. Over 40 percent of the consumer units surveyed in the early 1960s by the Bureau of Labor Statistics (BLS) in all areas except New York City and Portland, Maine, owned their own homes, and homeownership ranged as high as 69 percent for wage-earning and clerical families in Detroit and Buffalo. In New York, only 29 percent of all consumer units and 34 percent of wage-earning and clerical families owned a home, while 50 and 59 percent, respectively, owned a car. Auto ownership in other cities ranged from 64–85 percent for all consumer units to 77–96 percent for wage-earning and clerical families.[6]

The large percentage of families owning homes and automobiles is, in part, a reflection of the imperfect market for the rental and sale of durable goods. Take, for example, consumption of automobile services. In a perfect capital market, the owner of a car could consume the services of his car when he wished and rent his car or sell it when it was not in use. In an imperfect market, the payment the owner receives for renting his car is lower than the payment he must make to obtain an equivalent car from a dealer. Most consumers find that it is difficult to realize the value of durable goods except by consuming these goods themselves, and they find it expensive to

---

[5] *D. Hester and J. Tobin*, Studies in Portfolio Behavior *(New York: John Wiley & Sons, Inc., 1967), p. 4.*

[6] *U.S. Bureau of Labor Statistics*, Worker's Wealth and Family Living Standards, *BLS Report 238–1 (Washington, D.C.: U.S. Government Printing Office, December 1963), p. 682.*

consume durable goods without owning them. A second factor
may be the "conspicuous consumption" needs of families at
all income levels. Homes and cars are highly visible symbols
of success. Few people pin stock certificates to the walls of
their apartments, and few reveal their home mortgage terms
to neighbors!

A household's liquidity needs depend on its income level,
and so does its return on its investments. People with high
incomes own assets with greater income-producing potential
than those with low incomes. These assets take the form of
investments in private businesses, real estate, and stocks. And
high-income families often have access to inside information
on profitable investments, more frequent opportunities to participate in money-making ventures, and better credit at their
local bank.

All things considered, it seems reasonable to conclude that
people with high incomes are also likely to be those with large
assets. Of course the relationship is not perfect. Some high-
income families spend every nickel they earn. And some
inheritors depend on their assets for every bit of income. Nonetheless, earnings are an important source of assets, and we
should explore this relationship further.

WINDFALLS, FOUNDATIONS, AND
PURCHASING POWER

Windfalls such as gifts and inheritances are another source of
purchasing power. Windfalls are usually received by the very
rich, by an occasional winner of the New York State lottery,
and by a few other lucky individuals. A fairly small percentage
of the population gains assets from this source. The 1962
Federal Reserve Survey found, for example, that about 83
percent of all consumer units had *no* inherited assets. Of the
remaining 17 percent, only 5 percent inherited a substantial
portion of their assets. Nonetheless, among those with wealth
holdings of $500,000 or more (about 200,000 families), about
60 percent inherited assets.[7]

[7] Federal Reserve Survey, *p. 148.*

Windfalls are conducive to the accumulation of assets for several reasons: (1) The timing of most windfalls cannot be planned precisely. Thus at least a portion of windfall income will probably be saved while the recipient adjusts his spending decisions to reflect the new-found wealth. (2) Income from gifts and inheritances—the primary source of windfalls —is subject to lower tax rates than ordinary income, so more is available for the recipient to save after taxes. (3) Gifts and inheritances are often administered by the very accountants and lawyers whose skills helped build the family fortune in the first place. Thus some inheritors receive a double legacy of both money and talent.

Not all inheritances occur when the wealthy head of a household dies, though many people currently believe this is the time of reckoning. J. Paul Getty, one of *Fortune* magazine's two nominees for the world's richest man, directly inherited a mere $500,000 in his father's will. But his father's legacy was enormous. Says Getty, "I cannot honestly claim that I possessed any innate talent nor even any particular desire for a business career." Talked into trying his hand by his father, Getty received an advance of $100 a month for personal expenses plus funds for the purchase of low-cost leases and property. His big opportunity came in May 1916, when he and his father created Getty Oil Corporation. Of the 1,000 stock shares issued, 700 went to his father and 300 to him. From that moment Getty was destined to be a very wealthy man.[8]

Fortune has also published the names of the nation's 66 centimillionaires, who command assets of $150 million or more.[9] Many names on the list belong to financially prominent families who owe their position at the top to past accumulations of wealth. According to *Fortune*, the estimated combined net worth of four members of the Mellon family was between $1.7 and $3.3 billion, while three Du Ponts held between $500 and $700 million, and six Rockefellers held between $1.2 and $1.8 billion. Three Fords—Josephine, Benson, and William—

[8] J. Paul Getty, My Life and Fortune *(London: George Allen and Unwin Limited, 1964), pp. 55, 65, 122–129.*
[9] *"The Richest of the Rich," Fortune, 68, 5 (May 1968), 156.*

had estimated holdings of between $350 and $600 million. Of course, many other methods are available for disguising the true ownership of a company. For example, a firm owned by a wealthy family may be registered in the name of the family's attorney. Thus these figures probably understate the true value of family holdings. And the list is not all inclusive. For example, *Fortune* does not even mention Henry Ford II, though he is a man of substantial means.

Table 1

RELATIONSHIP BETWEEN INHERITED ASSETS AND
INCOME IN 1962

| | | | Percentage Distribution of Inherited Assets | | | |
| | | | | | Portion of Total Assets | |
1962 Income	All Units	Not Ascertained	None	Some	Small	Substantial
$0– 2,999	100		84	16	10	6
5,000– 7,499	100		84	16	12	4
10,000–14,999	100		84	16	11	5
15,000–24,999	100		73	27	21	6
25,000–49,999	100		58	42	34	8
50,000–99,999	100	3	71	26	12	14
100,000 and over	100	3	31	66	9	57

Source: Dorothy Projector and Gertrude Weiss, *Survey of Financial Characteristics of Consumers*, Federal Reserve Technical Papers, August 1966, p. 148.

The hand-in-hand relationship between income and assets is apparent in the *Federal Reserve Survey*. High-income consumer units inherit more assets than low-income units, and these inheritances constitute a larger share of the total assets of the former group. But this is not completely true, however, for the holdings of the $15,000–50,000 and the $50,000–100,000 income classes. Surprisingly, a larger percentage of those in the $15,000–50,000 group *inherit* assets; however, the assets inherited by those in the $50,000–100,000 group constitute a larger *portion* of total assets, suggesting that there may be two types of accumulated assets among families in this bracket.

The 14 percent with substantial inheritances probably receive a high income, in part because of their past accumulation of assets. The 71 percent with no inherited assets most likely have accumulated wealth out of their incomes.

There is no such ambiguity at the top! Over 66 percent of the consumer units with incomes of $100,000 or more have some inherited assets, and over 86 percent of these report that inheritances constitute a substantial portion of their total assets.

Until recently foundations provided yet another vehicle through which the wealthy could internalize the effects of programs designed to improve public welfare. Ostensibly foundations were set up to perform charitable acts. In return, the donors could use their contributions to reduce their gift and estate tax liabilities. In the case of some foundations, such as Ford and Rockefeller, these donations have usually been spent to foster worthwhile projects in education, science, and medicine. But many of the less well-known foundations were apparently established to provide "charity" to the donor and his family. Until the 1969 Tax Reform Act these donor-related charitable contributions were quite generous. For example, the J. M. Kaplan Fund, Inc., was granted an income tax exemption in 1946 based on its claim to be a charitable institution. Indeed it was! Over a period of time it accepted two notes from J. M. Kaplan, its founder, for $968,000 and $720 million, respectively. Kaplan offered *no* collateral for these loans and paid *no* interest. The notes were payable at his death.[10] Ordinary people can't eat their cake and have it too, but it seems that J. M. Kaplan could. Not only did he benefit from the tax deduction he took in setting up the foundation, but he borrowed back his money as well! Under the 1969 Tax Reform Act, Congress enacted a provision barring all donor-foundation dealings. This reduces the possibility that the rich will internalize the charity dispensed by their own foundations.

Until recently the incomes of foundations were not taxable, presumably because they were to be used for charitable pur-

---

[10] *Joseph Ruskay and Richard Osserman,* Halfway to Tax Reform *(Bloomington: University of Indiana Press, 1970), p. 37.*

poses. In a study of 534 foundations from 1961 to 1964, a congressional committee headed by Representative Wright Patman found that 111 of the foundations owned from 10 percent to 100 percent of the stock of major corporations in the United States. Yet less than half of all foundation receipts (income plus capital gains) were being paid out. Over time, large accumulations of wealth developed within the foundations. For example, the assets of the Rockefeller Foundation grew from $35.9 million in 1913 to more than $860 million in 1966, despite disbursements of over $1 billion. The assets of the Richard K. Mellon Foundation rose from $1,000 in 1947 to $121 million in 1964.[11] The relationship between receipts and contributions in 1968 for the 15 largest foundations is shown in Table 2.

The 1969 Tax Reform Act was designed to eliminate large asset accumulations by foundations. A foundation that does not spend most of its income for charitable or educational projects and fails to devote more than half its assets directly to such activities *must* spend all its current net income by turning it over to other charitable organizations or activities. The law makes special provision for long-term projects and for foundations with assets that yield little or no current income. It also imposes a tax of 4 percent on a foundation's net receipts.

Three years after the enactment of the 1969 reform, the foundations are still debating their responsiveness to the needs of the public. "Foundations," according to Orville G. Brim, Jr., former president of the Russell Sage Foundation, "operate with few, if any, reality checks. . . . Institutional isolationism breeds narcissism and illusory feelings of power and separates them from the frontiers of thought." Such charges are indeed serious considering the expenditures of $1.5–$2.0 billion that they make each year.[12] And if the large and well-known foundations operate in an atmosphere of isolation, how remote must be the thousands of less well-known foundations that list a post office box or a lawyer's office as their mailing address!

[11] *Ruskay and Osserman, p. 44.*
[12] The New York Times, *November 7, 1972.*

Table 2

ASSET HOLDINGS AND EARNINGS OF AMERICA'S 15
LARGEST FOUNDATIONS IN 1968*
(in Thousands)

Foundation	Market Value of Assets	Receipts	Contribution Paid Out	Ratio of Contribution Paid Out to Gross Receipts
Ford	$3,661,454	$278,323	180,233	64.8
Rockefeller	889,848	83,305	35,716	42.9
Duke	629,030	21,598	18,318	84.8
Lilly	579,660	6,829	6,881	100.6
Pew	541,342	6,582	8,297	126.1
Kellogg	436,406	15,688	13,612	86.8
Mott	413,296	17,091	12,157	71.1
Kresge	353,071	51,538	6,884	13.4
Hartford	351,930	16,634	16,503	99.2
Carnegie	334,642	15,618	11,882	76.1
Sloan	329,499	22,153	15,805	71.3
Longwood	226,149	6,984	3,860	55.3
Rockefeller Brothers	221,612	10,323	7,798	75.5
Houston	213,699	50,445	3,973	7.9
Moody	190,687	6,601	5,595	84.7

* The recent death of Robert Wood Johnson led to the receipt of over
$1.2 billion in assets by the foundation that bears his name. This made
the Johnson Foundation the second wealthiest in the United States.

Source: Staff Report of the Subcommittee on Domestic Finance of the
Committee on Banking and Currency, U.S. House of Representatives, "The
Fifteen Largest United States Foundations" (Washington, D.C.: U.S.
Government Printing Office, July 15, 1971), pp. 5, 9, 11, 23.

Foundations can exert a potentially great effect on our economic system, yet the exercise of that power has barely been
investigated. In thousands of instances foundations remain
the stepchildren of estate planners and tax advisers, very
effective tools through which the rich can decrease their tax
liabilities. We shall return to this point in Chapter 6.

INCOME AND EARNINGS

Generally speaking, people from wealthy homes find it easier to "make it," Horatio Alger and Hugh Hefner notwithstanding. If life is a great gamble, as some suggest, the odds are with the wealthy. Few things succeed in this world like success—one's own or one's parents'.

To see why this is so, we shall briefly discuss how labor is valued in the marketplace. A more detailed discussion of the relationship between education and income appears in chapters 9 and 10. Labor acquires market value, at least partially, because it is a factor in the production of goods and services that have value to consumers. Employers usually are not interested in rewarding a person for his innate qualities or providing for the happiness and financial security of mankind. The wages paid to an employee bear a relation to his contribution to output, and they are determined in the marketplace through the interaction of the forces of supply and demand. (There is evidence, however, that in noncompetitive industries a person's wages may be affected by his social status.) Since labor is not a homogeneous quantity, some workers earn more than others, and the process of wage determination is not a random one.

A person's earnings depend in part on the amount of human capital he possesses and on the price this capital commands in the marketplace. By human capital we mean the stock of talents, skills, and knowledge a person has accumulated. The greater his stock of human capital, the larger his earnings are likely to be. A person born with a knack for mathematics may have an edge over his peers, as may a skilled woodcutter, a talented artist, or a shrewd investor.

Investment in education represents a widely accepted way of acquiring increased human capital. The modern doctor, dentist, lawyer, and businessman accumulate knowledge both in the classroom and on the job. And many employers accept an educational degree as certification both of what one knows and of one's ability to persist in the face of great odds. Thus in 1971 the average elementary school graduate had an income of about $7,400 compared to incomes of $10,750 for the high school graduate and $16,700 for the person with four or more years of college study. These educational differentials have persisted over long periods of time.

Increasing human capital through schooling raises the likelihood that one will find a comfortable place in the income distribution—but does not guarantee it. There are many more people with low incomes than with low educational attainments, and the large number of people in the lower range of the income distribution cannot be explained either by the distribution of income or by innate intelligence.[13]

During the last century a few select colleges served as important wellsprings of human capital for the sons of the nation's rich. The growth of state universities and the development of loan and scholarship programs may have offset this to some extent, but other sources of human capital continue to differentiate the rich from the nonrich. One often overlooked fount is the vast amount of worldly wisdom acquired in the home. There is nothing in the American educational system that prepares a student for becoming wealthy, as Russell Baker aptly points out.

> Where, for example, do we go to learn how to get into tax-free municipals? I raise this particular question because of a conversation at lunch some years ago with a rich man. I had been complaining about having to borrow money from the bank to pay taxes.
> . . . "Get into tax-free municipals," he said.
> Now, there we were, talking like equals in this splendid restaurant. He had just disclosed an invaluable secret of the art of getting rich, yet at this crucial moment the deficiency of the American educational system created a chasm between us.
> Nobody had ever told me, you see, what tax-free municipals were.
> . . . to rich people, things like tax-free municipals are as commonplace as ski-lodges in Gstaad. To say, "I don't know what tax-free municipals are" would dumfound anybody who knows the least thing about billions. It

[13] *For a more detailed discussion of this point, see Christopher Jencks,* Inequality: A Reassessment of the Effect of Family and Schooling in America *(New York: Basic Books, Inc., Publishers, 1972).*

would be comparable to saying "what is a gstaad?"
. . . anyhow, even if you find out what tax-free
municipals are, you face the even more baffling problem
of how to get into them. Rich people inherit this kind of
knowledge. The old cliche about being born with a
silver spoon in the mouth has it all wrong; what the rich
are really born with is the secret of how to get into
tax-free municipals.[14]

Two individuals who are equally competent to do a particular job may nonetheless receive different salaries. Women
with the same schooling as men often earn less, on the average, for performing the same work. In 1969, for example,
males 25 years of age and over with four years or more of
college received a median income of approximately $12,250.
Females with the same schooling received about $5,800 and
Negro males received $8,560.[15] With a given level of schooling,
a man usually earns more in the city than in the country, more
in the North than in the South, and more with family contacts
than without. These earnings differences generally persist even
after work experience and educational quality differences are
taken into account. And, to no one's surprise, they frequently
work to the advantage of people from high-income homes.

Since imperfect information is an important source of earnings differences, the children of the wealthy may come out
ahead in the earnings race.[16] Information is imperfect precisely
because it is not readily available and obtaining it requires
effort. One must be able to afford the time not only to seek
out job opportunities but also to learn where to look. As Baker
suggests, there is a legacy of knowledge inherited by the
children of the successful.

The nonwealthy must conduct their own search for job
opportunities or pay an agency to find a job for them. When
a person discovers that he can make more money, either by

[14] *Russell Baker, "The Secret Weapon of Daddy Warbucks,"© 1971
by The New York Times Company. Reprinted by permission.*
[15] *U.S. Bureau of the Census, "Income in 1969 of Families and Persons
in the United States,"* Current Population Reports *(Washington, D.C.:
U.S. Government Printing Office, 1970), pp. 101, 104, 105.*
[16] *Of course, the children of the poor learn to excel in their own areas
of need. It is highly unlikely that the children of the wealthy would have
the knowledge required to survive "on the street."*

moving to another part of the country or by changing jobs, he must be able to afford the additional costs this involves. The man without assets of his own often finds it difficult to borrow and may be unable to move, whereas a person with liquid assets can be his own financier.

Of course, some might contend that this argument confuses the rich with the upper middle class. The rich need not look for jobs because their parents own the companies that will employ them. But the children of the rich do not always go to work for their families. Some may seek employment in such industries as publishing and investment banking, and for this group family background and a good education can open doors.

Imperfect markets may also provide special opportunities for the wealthy. Monopolies engaged in restricting supply generally aid those with high incomes by laying down stringent entrance requirements that frequently require the outlay of large sums of money. The American Medical Association, for example, not only has some measure of control over the number of medical schools in the country (thus decreasing price competition among schools), but also insists on a lengthy training period involving substantial investment costs.

Noncompetitive industries are frequently family-run and therefore provide an environment conducive to nepotism and cronyism. Although statistics are hard to come by, a study conducted in the late thirties indicated that a limited number of families held 50 percent or more ownership in such companies as A&P, Campbell Soup, Duke Power, Ford Motor, Gulf Oil, Koppers, Pittsburgh Coal, and S. M. Kress.[17] While the growth of conglomerates and the subsequent takeover threats have reduced the importance of family ownership in some parts of the economy, the companies just mentioned —and others like them—are more insulated against this trend than most. Moreover, the conglomerates have created wealth and power for a new class of financiers.

---

[17] *Temporary National Economic Committee, U.S. Securities and Exchange Commission*, Investigation of Concentration of Economic Power, *U.S. Senate, 76th Congress, 3d Session, Monograph No. 29 (Washington, D.C.: U.S. Government Printing Office), pp. 105–107.*

People who begin their careers with money are in a position to earn more during their lifetimes than those with equivalent amounts of human capital but without assets. Some redistribution of income may occur from the low-intelligence, low-motivation wealthy to the high-intelligence, high-motivation nonwealthy. And some children from wealthy homes may fall from grace. But on the whole, those who find the road to the top marked with golden signs find it harder to lose their way than those who must chart their own course.

PROPERTY CONCENTRATION AND THE WEALTH PYRAMID

The concentration of wealth in the United States is dramatically illustrated by the statistics compiled by the Federal Reserve Board for 1962. Consider first the relationship between size of assets and percentage of wealth held. Approximately 200,000 consumer units with assets of $500,000 or more own over 22 percent of the total wealth reported in the *Federal Reserve Survey* and 32 percent of the investment assets.[18] The next 500,000 units, with assets valued at $200,000–500,000, own about 13 percent of the wealth and 22 percent of the investment assets. By adding an additional 700,000 units worth $100,000–200,000, we can account for 43 percent of the total wealth and 65 percent of the investment assets.[19] Yet these 1.4 million consumer units made up only about 2 percent of the total households in the United States in 1962![20]

[18] *By investment assets we mean publicly traded stock, marketable securities other than stock, mortgage assets, investment real estate, business investments not managed by the consumer unit, and company savings plans.*

[19] Federal Reserve Survey, pp. 151, 136.

[20] *Professor Robert Lampman points out that this finding is inconsistent with his estimate that the top 2 percent of families held 28.5 percent of total private wealth in 1953. (See Robert Lampman, The Share of Top Wealthholders in National Wealth [Princeton, N.J.: Princeton University Press, 1962], p. 24.) The major reason for this seems to be the exclusion of life insurance and annuity and retirement plans asserts from the Federal Reserve figures. Assets of this type are more likely to be held by smaller estates and not directly related to the issue of property concentration because they are not under the control of their future owners.*

An even more dramatic example of the concentration of property may be seen if the data on wealth are grouped by income level. Figure 2 is drawn so that the wealth holdings of those with the highest incomes are shown at the bottom of the pyramid. The diagram is drawn to scale, and each block shows an income interval. The data are derived from the same statistics used to prepare Figure 1. Notice the surprisingly large amount of wealth held by the 700,000 consumer units with incomes of $25,000 or more. And note the towering amount of wealth held by the negligible number of units with incomes of over $100,000. These relationships usually are not available to the public because no government agency collects and publishes annual data on wealth.

Figure 2
AVERAGE AMOUNT OF WEALTH HELD
BY INCOME GROUPS

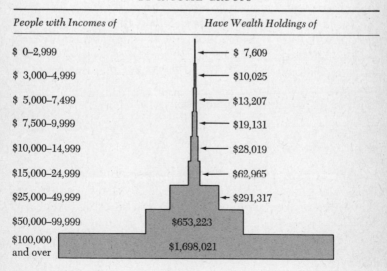

People with Incomes of	Have Wealth Holdings of
$ 0–2,999	$ 7,609
$ 3,000–4,999	$10,025
$ 5,000–7,499	$13,207
$ 7,500–9,999	$19,131
$10,000–14,999	$28,019
$15,000–24,999	$62,965
$25,000–49,999	$291,317
$50,000–99,999	$653,223
$100,000 and over	$1,698,021

Source: Dorothy Projector and Gertrude Weiss, *Survey of Financial Characteristics of Consumers*, Federal Reserve Technical Papers, August 1966, p. 110.

DEMOGRAPHY AND THE ACCUMULATION PROCESS

Patterns of birth, marriage, and death may either support or counteract the forces leading to concentration of wealth. If the rich have more children than the nonrich, they will spread their wealth among more people and thus reduce their share relative to the rest of the population. The reverse is also true: If the rich have fewer children than the nonrich, this will increase their share of the nation's property. In fact, however, there is little evidence that over the long run birth patterns aid in or detract from the accumulation of wealth in the United States.

The same cannot be said for attitudes toward marriage. If the selection of marriage partners occurred randomly, there would be an even chance that rich people would marry poor people and vice versa. Over time, marriage would serve to equalize inheritances. In fact, however, most marriages occur between people of similar backgrounds, and the wealthy usually choose their spouses from their own ranks. A glance at the social page of *The New York Times* illustrates how common assortative marriage actually is—high-income women marry high-income men, college graduates seek each other out, professional men frequently marry the daughters of professional men, and so on. Marriage patterns raise an important barrier to property equalization.

A MATTER OF ATTITUDES

Social attitudes may contribute to the perpetuation of inequality. If the rich are taught to believe in their own superiority, they will probably be opposed to policies that bring them closer to the masses. Similarly, if the poor believe they are not as good as the rich—be it in terms of education or of breeding— they may have no incentive to alter their position in the income distribution. Some sociologists like to refer to the stratified character of society and to emphasize occupational differences as the source of differing class attitudes. Others have stressed the reinforcing nature of the social stratification process as a kind of reward system to people in better jobs.

Social status is then treated as a nonpecuniary reward for success.[21]

The role of social attitudes is highlighted in this passage from *Social Mobility in Industrial Society*, by Lipset and Bendix:

> Occupational and social status are to an important
> extent self-perpetuating. They are associated with many
> factors which make it difficult for individuals to modify
> their status. Position in the social structure is
> usually associated with a certain level of income,
> education, family structure, community reputation and so
> forth. These become part of a vicious circle in which each
> factor acts on the other in such a way as to preserve
> the social structure in its present form.[22]

Not all sociologists would agree with this statement. Objections have been raised about the *cumulative* effect of background factors. For example, Otis Dudley Duncan and Peter Blau agree that while the relationship between background and social mobility is not trivial, "it is not great enough in itself to justify a conception of a system that insures a circle of poverty or wealth." They argue that the presence of several related determinants of social position creates a redundant, not a cumulative, effect and deny that the research done so far provides a real insight into the process of social mobility.[23]

Americans are proud of their wealth and of their wealthy. An erstwhile philosopher is said to have remarked, "We are all affluent now." To possess a great store of wealth is part of the American dream, and as long as there is the slightest chance of "making it," the middle class will probably pay homage to their wealthier cousins.

Moreover, the difference in the standard of living for those with large asset holdings as compared with those of moderate

[21] *Kingsley Davis and Wilbert E. Moore,* "Some Principles of Stratification," The American Sociological Review, *10, 2 (April 1945), 242–249.*

[22] *Seymour Martin Lipset and Reinhard Bendix,* Social Mobility in Industrial Society *(Berkeley: University of California Press, 1959), pp. 198–199.*

[23] *Peter Blau and Otis Dudley Duncan,* The American Occupational Structure *(New York: John Wiley & Sons, Inc., 1967), p. 203.*

holdings has narrowed substantially through time. First, the
increase in the number of possessions held by the average man
has made differences in property holdings less offensive. A
reasonably prosperous Roman family owned about 500 articles. By contrast, a 1939 study found over 1,500 articles then
in use in an average American family, and the number has
probably skyrocketed since.[24] Second, even where differences
in *quantity* exist, *quality* differences have become less important and the average family is both willing and able to commit
its income before it is received. It seems unlikely that a low-
income family paying off its $300 portable color-television set
over ten years will march in the streets to protest the special
privileges of the high-income person who can pay cash for a
$600 console. Besides, once the set is purchased both must
choose from the same program fare.

The more glaring class differences are increasingly covered
up in today's world. In 1962, Harrington pointed out that
"America has the best dressed poverty the world has ever
known. . . . In Detroit, the existence of social classes became
much more difficult to discern the day companies put lockers
in the plants. From that moment on, one did not see men in
work clothes on the way to the factory, but citizens in slacks
and white shirts."[25] Since then, Levi Strauss has replaced
Brooks Brothers and casual dress has become the almost universal symbol of the younger generation.

The very rich have also changed their habits. As G. William
Domhoff suggests, social institutions are the backbone of the
modern leisure class—"private schools, elite universities, and
'right' fraternities, gentleman's clubs, debutante balls, summer resorts, and cultural organizations."[26] The giant castles of
the past have been replaced by tasteful high-rise apartments
and secluded summer homes, and today's "jet set" includes
numerous singers, actors, novelists, and other Johnny-come-
latelys.

[24] *Robert Rutherford Doane*, The Anatomy of American Wealth *(New
York: Harper & Row, Publishers, Inc., 1940), p. 53.*
[25] *Michael Harrington*, The Other America *(Baltimore, Md.: Penguin
Books, 1963), pp. 12–13.*
[26] *G. William Domhoff*, Who Rules America *(Englewood Cliffs, N.J.:
Prentice-Hall, Inc., 1967), p. 16.*

Unlike the conspicuous consumption described by Thorstein Veblen, we now seem to be experiencing a new type of behavior that might be called *privatization* of wealth. It is no longer necessary for the old rich to enjoy their incomes through the eyes (and looks) of others. They have learned to live with it. Moreover, the new rich are increasingly emerging from the business community and are preoccupied with other matters. Today's wealthy are probably more likely than those of earlier times to wear golf shoes rather than patent leather and to travel tourist rather than first class. By removing their spending from public view, by living in separate areas and socializing in secluded spots, they reduce public awareness and—indirectly—hostility. For the wealthy of the turn of the century, a high income bought publicity; for the wealthy of the seventies it buys privacy.

The average American probably looks up to Jacqueline Kennedy Onassis for her style of life rather than her money. And Howard Hughes, Hugh Hefner, and J. Paul Getty are more than just wealthy men; they are personifications of the American dream. Should our standard of living be great enough by 2025 so that the average American could live like Howard Hughes, there would probably still be some who would look to the top of the income distribution with the same reverence that we find today.

THE WAR FOR WEALTH

Back in 1871 John Stuart Mill provided the following definition of wealth:

> We really, and justly, look upon a person as possessing
> the advantages of wealth, not in proportion to the useful
> and agreeable things of which he is in the actual enjoy-
> ment, but to his command over the general fund of things
> useful and agreeable; the power he possesses of providing
> for any exigency, or obtaining any object of desire.[27]

As Mill so aptly points out, wealth is a source of power, which manifests itself in several ways. Political power accrues

[27] *John Stuart Mill*, Principles of Political Economy, *1871 ed., p. 3.*

to the wealthy through campaign contributions, the hiring of
lobbyists, and access to government appointments to regulatory agencies, foreign embassies, and the like. Economic
power results from holdings of large amounts of stock in key
companies, from directorships of banks and corporate boards
of directors, and from foundations and other devices that
enable the select few to maintain control of large companies.
A special power accrues to the rich as a result of their identification with the "best" interests of the nation. All of these
forms of power lead to the internalization of economic gains
to the benefit of the wealthy. And all make it difficult to interrupt the process of wealth accumulation. For no sooner is a
new program proposed than a new method is found by which
the wealthy may benefit. Provide a medicare program and
watch doctors' profits grow; build new schools and observe the
increasing prosperity of large contractors; create a federal
housing program and develop a new class of wealthy property
owners. The list is almost as large as the resources that the
wealthy bring to bear on their task.

The wealthy are in a unique position to defend their interests, and they have done so with great aplomb. Using the
various tools at their disposal they have fought, and continue
to fight, a "war for wealth." It is an enterprising war fought
in support of the principle of internalization of wealth. Sometimes it attacks socialism; at other times it advocates it. It
opposes negative taxes for the poor but favors them for the
rich. Its chief motto seems to be "to him that gets, give." And
the enemies in the war are those who seek a more equitable
distribution of income.

The war for wealth has shaped our tax laws, expenditure
programs, and lending and borrowing institutions. To understand this war we need to know more about its combatants.
Who are the wealthy and what are their weapons? Who are
their allies and in what arenas are the battles fought and won?
These are the subjects of future chapters.

2
THE AFFLUENT MINORITY

F. Scott Fitzgerald: You know, Ernest,
the rich are different from us.
Ernest Hemingway: Yes, I know. They
have more money than we do.

Who are the affluent? The answer depends on whom you ask. Herman Miller examines the wealthiest 5 percent of American families in his well-known book *Rich Man Poor Man*. He finds that they are usually the well educated: "The small businessman and the farmer have given way to the engineer, scientist, college professor, plant manager, and others who deal primarily with ideas, not things."[1] Others take a different point of view. Says Ferdinand Lundberg, ". . . the day of accumulating gargantuan new personal fortunes in the United States is just about ended; this leaves the tubbed, scrubbed, and public relations anointed inheritors of the nineteenth-century money scramble holding most of the chips."[2] And according to C. Wright Mills, "Wealth does not center in any personality. To be celebrated, to be wealthy, to have power requires access to major institutions . . ."[3]

No single definition of affluence will be acceptable to all. If affluence is measured by the satisfaction of people, some with high incomes will be judged very poor while others with low incomes will be considered quite rich. If affluence is measured by the quality of living conditions, standards must be estab-

---

[1] *Herman Miller*, Rich Man Poor Man *(New York: Thomas Y. Crowell Company, 1971)*, p. 132.
[2] *Ferdinand Lundberg*, The Rich and the Super Rich *(New York: Bantam Books, Inc., 1969)*, p. 35.
[3] The Power Elite *(New York: Random House, Inc., 1963)*, pp. 5–6.

lished to show when one person is better off than another. In
either event, the dividing line between a moderate standard
of living and an affluent one is likely to be subjective.

At the very top of the income distribution are the inheritors
plus a few wealthy oil tycoons. Here are the "generals" in
the war for wealth, busily engaged in directing new campaigns
or living out their golden years in unparalleled luxury. Beneath
them in the pyramid, but within sight of the top, are a few
top business executives, real-estate operators, and professional
men. And still further down are those described by Herman
Miller—the engineer, scientist, small businessman, and farmer.

In this chapter we undertake a journey to the top of the
income distribution. The journey begins at what we label the
"threshold of affluence"—that is, the income level that is just
sufficient to meet the average family's reasonable needs. Several successive way stations along the road to riches are then
explored, and the occupants of each station are identified and
discussed. In the process, several shortcomings of income distribution figures are discussed and their effects on income
distribution explored.

A REASONABLE DEFINITION OF AFFLUENCE

We begin our search for a reasonable definition of affluence
with the assertion that a family is affluent when it is at least
able to fulfill its basic needs. This raises several difficult questions if one wishes to identify a threshold of affluence. In order
for a family that enjoys eating to cross the threshold, must it
have an income sufficiently high so that it can pay for a well-
prepared beef Wellington? Should that family be able to send
its children to Ivy League schools or buy separate cars for its
children? No objective answer can be given to these questions.
But as long as we are willing to accept average tastes, a
threshold can be found. At a bare minimum, the affluent family
must fulfill its biological needs. It should be adequately fed,
decently clothed, and comfortably sheltered. It ought to have
money for reasonable amounts of recreation and travel and to
be able to provide for its foreseeable health needs. By these

basic standards of adequacy, a surprising number of Americans are not affluent.

No *single* income provides a threshold between comfort and affluence. Therefore we shall look at several bench-mark incomes established by various federal agencies. Best known of these is the poverty line proposed by the Social Security Administration (SSA). Using prevailing food prices and a set of dietary requirements prepared by the U.S. Department of Agriculture (USDA), the SSA computes the minimum cost of providing nutritious meals for a family for one year. Yearly food costs are then multiplied by three on the assumption that low-income families spend one-third of their total income on food. The resulting figure, frequently referred to as the poverty line, was $3,743 for an urban family of four in 1969.[4] This figure is updated each year to take account of inflation.

Unfortunately, the poverty line fails to provide a realistic dividing line between poverty and adequacy. For one thing, it presupposes a talent for home economics that few housewives possess. A 1965 study by the Department of Agriculture showed, for example, that more than 60 percent of all households with incomes under $13,000 had inadequate diets. For another, the budget used has not been updated since 1959. Even its designers refer to it as a temporary budget for short-run use. A more realistic standard of $6,567 is provided for a middle-aged urban worker with a family of four by the Bureau of Labor Statistics (BLS). This budget is based on USDA nutritional requirements and information on the actual expenditures made by families as revealed in consumer expenditure surveys. It is designed to permit a standard of living "sufficient to provide for the health, social well-being, the nurture of children, and participation in community activities for an urban family of four."

The BLS low-income budget provides a more generous living standard than the one defined by the poverty line. The budget breaks down as follows: food, 26 percent; housing, 22

[4] *U.S. Bureau of the Census, "Selected Characteristics of Persons and Families,"* Current Population Reports, *Series P-20, No. 204 (Washington, D.C.: U.S. Government Printing Office, March 1970).*

percent; direct taxes, 9 percent; other basic needs, 43 percent. Only 5 percent, or $320, is available for recreation and other consumption expenditures. Yet even at this income level many families cannot adjust their shopping patterns and culinary skills to achieve the economies envisioned by the designers of this standard. The BLS estimates that only one-fourth of the families spending the amounts recommended by the plan will have adequate diets because "menus based on this plan will include foods requiring a considerable amount of home preparation as well as skill in cooking to make varied and appetizing meals."[5]

A third bench mark is provided by the moderate or average budget prepared by the BLS. An urban family of four living on this budget—equal to $10,077 in 1969—would probably lead a fairly comfortable existence. Compared to that of people living on the low-income budget just described, their diet consists of more meat, fish, and fresh vegetables. They live in better housing and have more money for recreation and travel. Somewhere between this expenditure level and the BLS low-income budget, the family's standard of living begins to resemble that of the middle class.

The BLS also defines a more generous standard—equal to $14,589 in 1969—that assumes families eat a greater variety of foods, live in more expensive housing, purchase better transportation and clothing, and spend more on recreation and travel. About 19 percent of family income goes for food, 24 percent for housing, 11 percent for clothing and personal care, 8 percent for transportation, and 17 percent for direct taxes. If the sole criterion for affluence is whether a family can meet its reasonable needs, urban families of four with incomes greater than $15,000 in 1969 have crossed the threshold.

Several other estimates have been prepared that indicate the affluence threshold for urban families differing in size and composition from the four-person urban-worker family. The standard for each type of family is shown in Table 3. On the

[5] U.S. *Bureau of Labor Statistics*, 3 Standards of Living for an Urban Family of Four Persons, *Bulletin No. 1570–5 (Washington, D.C.: U.S. Government Printing Office, Spring 1967).*

Table 3

AFFLUENCE THRESHOLDS FOR URBAN FAMILIES OF
DIFFERENT SIZES, TYPES, AND AGES, SPRING 1969

Family*	Threshold
Four-Person Urban-Worker Family	$10,804
Single Person Under Age 35	3,780
Husband-Wife Under Age 35	
No Children	5,290
1 Child Under Age 6	6,700
2 Children, Older Under 6	7,780
Husband-Wife, Age 35–54	
1 Child 6–15	8,860
2 Children, Older 6–15	10,804
3 Children, Oldest 6–15	12,530
Husband and Wife Retired, 65 or Older	5,811
Single Person Retired, 65 or Older	3,200

*The careful reader will note that these estimates are not exactly com-
parable with those used in the text. The BLS does not include in these
figures payments for gifts and contributions, life insurance, occupational
expenses, social security, and direct taxes. The allowance made for direct
taxes alone in the $14,589 budget is $2,523.

Source: *Monthly Labor Review*, 93, 4 (April 1970), 62.

basis of these figures, we estimate that probably no more than
one-third of the U.S. population had incomes sufficient to reach
the threshold of affluence in 1969.

MY SATISFACTION AND YOUR SATISFACTION

The use of an income-determined line to define the threshold
of wealth ignores an important source of satisfaction to the
wealthy—namely, the *status* associated with high income or
substantial asset holdings. Economists have long assumed that
one consumer's wants are independent of another's, but they
have yet to persuade consumers of this fact. Emulation plays
an important role both in the process of want creation and in
determining one's status in the community.

Our notions of affluence and poverty are based on relative
rather than absolute criteria. The leader of the Masai tribe in

Africa is considered rich by his fellow tribesmen, even though both his income and his standard of living are meager by American standards. Compared to other tribesmen he is a wealthy man. In America, however, contemporary mores and the beguilements of advertising encourage people to compare their possessions with their neighbors' and to feel deprived if their own goods are inferior. A $350 color TV set often yields greater satisfaction to its owner if his neighbor has a black-and-white set than if the neighbor has a $600 color console.

Because consumer wants are interdependent, the satisfaction a person receives from his own income is not independent of other people's incomes. We can illustrate the implications of this with a simple diagram. Suppose that the only source of satisfaction from income is one's standing relative to the rest of the community. Suppose, too, that as one's income increases relative to his peers', his satisfaction increases at a decreasing rate. Then the relationship between relative income and satisfaction may be illustrated by a curve such as 00. An increase in a family's income relative to the community income implies a move to the right along the curve and an increase in its satisfaction. This is shown in Figure 3.

Figure 3
RELATIVE SATISFACTION OF FAMILIES

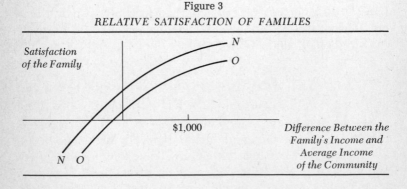

Why might a high-income family living in a high-income community not feel more satisfied with its income than a lower-income family in a lower-income community? Assume that both families derive the same satisfaction from a given *relative* income difference (i.e., *00* is the same for the two families). If one family makes a posttax income of $10,000 in a community with a mean income of $9,000 and the other makes a posttax income of $14,000 in a community with a mean income of $13,000, they will both receive the same amount of satisfaction. Even though one family's income is closer to the biological comfort line, its satisfactions, viewed *solely* on a relative basis, are no greater than the other family's. Thus increases in community income can offset increases in a family's income. An increase of $1,000 in both family and community income leaves the family at the same point on the curve as before.

More realistically, a family receives satisfaction both from its current standard of living and from its status relative to the rest of the community. Suppose that we now let *00* represent the satisfaction a family receives from an income of $10,000 in a community with a mean income of $9,000 and let *NN* represent the satisfaction received at an income level of $14,000 in a community with a mean income of $13,000. A movement outward along either curve shows the satisfaction experienced by a family as community income falls relative to its own income. For any given relative income difference—$1,000 in our example—the satisfaction received increases as income increases, reflecting the fact that a family with a high income can achieve a higher standard of living than one with a low income.

A high-income family may grow discontented with its income for several reasons. If community income increases while its own stays the same, the family will feel itself sliding down the satisfaction curve to the left and will be less contented than before. Moreover, since families usually have an imperfect knowledge of community income, they must rely on ad hoc data, such as personal knowledge of their friends' possessions, to gauge their relative status in the community. The greater the number of contacts with families whose standard of living is higher than their own, the more discontented they are likely to become. This may help explain the growing trend toward privatization of wealth. By adopting a style of inconspicuous consumption, the rich reduce the potential dissatisfaction that their wealth might otherwise create.

Some readers may be puzzled as to why a family would want to move to a wealthy community if comparisons with its new neighbors might make it feel worse off. The explanation may be that wealthy areas provide an environment that may be highly satisfying—relatively crime-free streets, good public facilities, a more prestigious address, a touch of greenery, and the like. The decision to move is usually based on an evaluation of the benefits and costs of such a move.

Moreover, a family that moves into a new community does not make contact with its neighbors immediately. During the transition period it is likely to compare its standard of living to the standard prevailing in the neighborhood it has left behind. Such comparisons probably lead to a short-term gain in satisfaction. Since many families move to "better" communities in anticipation of rising income, long-term satisfaction is also obtainable if family income rises more rapidly than that of the community.

THE ROAD TO RICHES

It should now be clear that the road to riches has several way stations and that a single commonly agreed upon definition of affluence is hard to find. Nonetheless, it seems clear that if $9,800 is the median income in the United States, a family with $50,000 is well along the road to riches, and one with an income of $500,000 is exceptionally affluent. Thus, following Hemingway's suggestion that to find the rich we must look for people with money, we shall identify the wealthy in several stages based on how much income they receive.

According to the Census Bureau, the U.S. population was 200.2 million in March 1970. Of this number, 51.2 million headed families, another 134.2 million resided in those families, and the remaining 14.8 million lived alone or in households in which they had no relations. Using data on the pretax money incomes of those families in 1969, the Census Bureau reported that roughly 8 million had incomes slightly above the affluence threshold—that is, in the $15,000–24,000 range. Another 1.6 million families had incomes between $25,000 and $50,000, while only 205,000 had incomes of $50,000 or more. The remaining 41.4 million had incomes below the threshold of affluence.[6]

If families and unrelated individuals are added together to form consumer units, the income pyramid described earlier is barely affected: 8.26 million consumer units have incomes between $15,000 and $25,000, 1.7 million receive incomes between $25,000 and $50,000, and 210,000 have incomes of $50,000 or more.

Families in the $15,000–25,000 income bracket may be thought of as members of the "estate class." Under the federal tax laws an estate tax is levied on a person's estate only if it exceeds $60,000. Since the average wealth held by a consumer unit in this group is about $63,000, the title "estate class" seems fitting. Of course, not all families with incomes of $15,000 have assets of $60,000, and vice versa. Families in the second group are called "knights" in recognition of their role in the war for wealth. The third group—consisting of both the rich and the very rich—have been dubbed "warlords" in deference to their position at the top of the income pyramid. Since these three groups constitute the vanguard of the war for wealth, it is important to get a clearer picture of them.

The Estate Class

The characteristics of families in the estate class differ only slightly from national norms. The median age of a family head in this group is 46.8 years, and over 75 percent of the heads of families are between the ages of 24 and 54. The median number of school years completed by a family head is 12.8 compared to 12.2 for the nation.[7] Estate class families are 95 percent white and 95 percent consist of both a husband and wife.[8] A surprising number of estate class families send women to work—52 percent compared to a national figure of 34 percent. The 15.6 percent of all families who are members of the estate class receive 14.5 percent of the wage and salary income,

[6] U.S. Bureau of the Census, "Income in 1969 of Families and Persons in the United States," Current Population Reports, Series P-60, No. 75 (Washington, D.C.: U.S. Government Printing Office, 1970) p. 32. Hereafter referred to as Census Bureau Report.

[7] Census Bureau Report, p. 19.

[8] Census Bureau Report, p. 22.

7.1 percent of the nonfarm self-employment income, and 2.1 percent of the farm self-employment income reported to the Census Bureau.[9] These figures suggest that relatively few estate class wage earners are self-employed as compared to those above them, and very few are farmers.

Members of the estate class generally reside in metropolitan areas and make up almost 19 percent of the population of these areas. Many families prefer the suburbs, however; as a result, the estate class constitutes 21.2 percent of the metropolitan population outside central cities.[10] These families are prime targets for appliance dealers, automobile salesmen, and real-estate brokers.

By the standards just discussed, the estate group is close enough to the *threshold* of affluence so that it can hardly be singled out for its lush living. Yet estate class families rank among the staunchest supporters of the war for wealth. Several factors may account for this. First, having tasted some affluence the estate class would like more. Since those at the top of the income distribution serve as a model for emulation, members of the estate class frequently accept the policies proposed by those above them, all too often failing to recognize that their interests are not the same as those of people higher up in the income distribution. We shall present several poignant examples of this in the tax discussion in chapters 6 and 7.

Second, some policies advocated in the war for wealth involve financing schemes that require people near the bottom of the income distribution to pay proportionately more in taxes. For example, most states finance their expenditures through sales and excise taxes. In many instances these taxes place a disproportionate burden on people with low and middle incomes. Precisely because sales taxes take a proportionately greater amount of tax from those with low incomes, the gap between the lower-middle and upper-middle income groups increases after taxes. As a result, the less altruistic estate class members may feel better off relative to those with lower incomes (i.e., they move to the right along the *00* curve in Figure 3). In other

---

[9] Census Bureau Report, *pp. 80–81.*
[10] Census Bureau Report, *p. 32.*

words, their quest for status leads estate class members to support regressive tax policies.

Finally, the war for wealth often has a direct effect on estate class pocketbooks. For example, many engineers and scientists in this class find it necessary to defend the nation's military policies in order to ensure their own job security. Over the years these people have come to realize that the nation's commitment to defense is greater than its commitment to full employment. Ironically, a strange communality of interests develops between the $50,000 entrepreneur who depends on the military for profits and the $16,000 employee of a defense company who wants to keep his job. This process of *identification*, like that of internalization, strengthens the position of the very rich, and it also gives them the resources needed to fight the war for wealth.

The Knights

At the second way station on the road to riches rest the 1.6 million families with gross incomes between $25,000 and $50,000. The knight heads of families—median age 50.4—are almost four years older on the average than heads of families of the estate class, and more of them are over the age of 54. As befits a member of the privileged class, a knight is better educated than those beneath him: The median number of school years completed by a family head is 15.6, compared to the national average of 12.2.

About 97 percent of the families with incomes between $25,000 and $50,000 are white, and 96 percent include both a husband and a wife. Only 41 percent of these families send women into the labor force—about 12 percent less than in the estate class. The knights make up 3.2 percent of all American families and receive 2.2 percent of all wage and salary income, 4.7 percent of nonfarm self-employment income, and 0.5 percent of farm self-employment income. Whereas about 30 percent of the families in the estate class report income derived solely from earnings, only 18 percent of the knights rely solely on earnings.[11] And an examination of occupational data confirms

[11] Census Bureau Report, *p. 66.*

Herman Miller's view that professional and managerial occupations are well represented in the higher reaches of the
income distribution. Many occupants of this group are self-
employed or managerial workers in the construction, manu-
facturing, or real-estate industries. Relatively few are in
agriculture or trade industries.

Families in this income group tend to be city dwellers, and
they live in conditions of relative affluence. Commenting on
the results of a national survey of 16,171 adults conducted in
1967, one writer for *Fortune* states:

> . . . something thoroughly satisfying happens to people
> when they cross an income threshold of around
> $25,000 a year. Until then basic family wants tend to
> outrun income, but afterward income moves ahead
> of needs. The family pays off debts and stays out of debt.
> And major costs are met from current income. Most
> families find that even sending children to college is
> not financially binding.[12]

People with incomes between $25,000 and $75,000 are three
times as likely to own a color-television set or hi-fi components
as those with incomes of less than $15,000, five times as likely
to serve Scotch, and seven times as likely to drink four or more
glasses of imported wine in a week. In other words, they have
the freedom to purchase luxury goods. And since few people
have such freedom, these are truly the elite members of our
society.

The Warlords

At the top of the income distribution sit the "warlords," 210,-
000 consumer units strong—200,000 families and 10,000 single
individuals. Rarely have so few been so well hidden from the
public. For despite the piles of income statistics that have been
accumulated as a result of our national concern with poverty,
most statisticians, until recently, have lumped together all
incomes over $15,000. The breakdown of income categories in

[12] *Jeremy Main, "Good Living Begins at $25,000 a Year," Fortune,
67, 5 (May 1968), 160.*

the Census Bureau Report *Income in 1969 of Families and Persons in the United States* enables us to catch a glimpse of the income peak. Our study of the families with incomes of $50,000 or more still provides a misleading picture of the top, however, because it disguises the difference between the rich and the very rich. Thus we shall be forced to gather additional data to highlight the characteristics of those at the very top.

Warlords differ somewhat from those immediately below them. The average warlord family head has almost one year more of education than his average knight counterpart. He is also likely to be the same age as the knight. Slightly more than 98 percent of the warlord families are white, and most are Protestant—although there is little evidence that pursuit of the "Protestant ethic" helped them reach the top. Barely 23 percent of the wives of families in this group work; family assets are substantially greater than the assets of those in the lower income brackets.

In the $50,000–100,000 income group we find professional men (chiefly lawyers and doctors), business executives, farmers, druggists, contractors, and salesmen. According to preliminary statistics from the Internal Revenue Service (IRS), in 1970 about 351,700 income tax returns were filed by people with adjusted incomes in this range.

Two factors help account for the discrepancy between the IRS and Census Bureau figures—underreporting of income and the tax laws. Underreporting occurs primarily because the Census Bureau obtains its series on money income by asking people to estimate their incomes. Frequently the figures obtained in this manner are substantially lower than those acquired when families consult actual records. Underreporting is further compounded by the fact that the Census Bureau does not include certain items such as gains realized from the sale of stocks in its definition of income. Moreover, the tax laws encourage some families to file more than one tax return. But more about this later.

Although there are several problems involved in using IRS figures, these data are an important source of information on the incomes of the most affluent members of our society. Of the

429,568 returns reporting adjusted gross incomes[13] of $50,000 or more in 1970, 351,669, or 81.9 percent, had incomes between $50,000 and $100,000; 62,576, or 14.6 percent, reported incomes of $100,000–200,000; 12,930, or 3 percent, had incomes of $200,000–500,000; 1,769, or 0.4 percent, listed incomes between $500,000 and $1 million; and 624, or only 0.1 percent, had incomes of $1 million or more.[14]

Here is the income pyramid in all its glory! *Fortune*'s 1970 survey of the heads of the 500 largest corporations found that although most top executives are very handsomely paid, few have gross annual incomes over $400,000. More than half of those surveyed reported that earnings were 80 percent or more of their income, and stock options notwithstanding, more than half had a *net worth* of less than $1 million.[15] The incomes of the presidents of 40 large corporations are shown in Table 4. Both the size and the composition of presidential incomes differ significantly by company and relatively few incomes exceed the $1 million mark. Nonetheless, most of the individuals on this list make more income in five years than an "executive" earning $15,000 a year grosses in a lifetime.

How many of the 624 tax returns of $1 million or more come from the businessmen listed in Table 4? To answer this question we shall reexamine the IRS data. A striking fact about the sources of revenue for those with incomes of $1 million or more is that only about 7 percent of their reported income comes from wages and salaries. The average income in this class is $2.1 million. Of this amount, about $89,000 is wage and salary income; adding in other earnings sources such as partnership income increases this figure only to about $108,000. Dividends received amount to $851,000 or 40 percent of reported income, and interest adds another 6 percent. Without doubt the major income source for those in this income group

[13] *The term "adjusted gross income" is used by the Treasury to denote the income that is subject to taxation under the individual income tax. It excludes such items as interest on tax-exempt state and local bonds, costs of work related to travel away from home, and a limited range of educational expenses if necessary for a person to keep his job.*

[14] *U.S. Treasury,* Preliminary Statistics of Income, 1970 *(Washington, D.C.: U.S. Government Printing Office, 1972), p. 22.*

[15] *Robert S. Diamond, "A Self-Portrait of the Chief Executive: The Fortune-Yankelovich Survey,"* Fortune, 81, 5 *(May 1970), 181.*

is capital gains income. About 485 returns (78 percent of the total) reported capital gains that totaled $620 million. This amounted to an average capital gain of almost $995,000 per return!

Harold Geneen, the highest-paid executive on our list, received an average $1.1 million in capital gains each year. Geneen, president and chairman of the board of International Telephone & Telegraph, earned a salary of over $356,700 and received other compensation of $410,000. With profits up about 20 percent in 1970, Geneen exercised stock options worth $1.9 million, for which he paid $1.1 million. His total income in 1970 exceeded $1.5 million, somewhat less than the average income reported to the IRS for those in the $1 million-and-over tax bracket.

Many other executives were not quite as fortunate. In 1970 the president of Ford Motor received slightly more than $639,000, including options, while the president of Chase Manhattan Corp. earned about $184,000. H. I. Romnes, president and chairman of American Telephone & Telegraph, was paid only about $356,000, and Milo Brisco, president of Exxon Corp., averaged about $330,000. Although corporations provide an important access route to the top of the income distribution, it would appear that very few corporation presidents travel the road all the way.

Who files the 0.1 percent of all returns with $1 million or more? The IRS statistics suggest that the people in the top income bracket are those who own substantial assets and whose income is derived primarily from dividends and capital gains. In other words, those with the highest incomes are *not* those with the highest earnings but rather those with a substantial accumulation of assets! The last chapter explored the sources of accumulated wealth and showed that a major source of wealth is inheritance. This point is brought out dramatically in Table 5, which lists the 66 top centimillionaires in the United States in 1967 according to *Fortune* magazine. Although some may disagree about whether specific individuals belong on the list, one thing is quite clear: A substantial number of individuals with the largest assets and therefore with the largest capital gains incomes are inheritors. And with several

Table 4

COMPENSATION OF SELECTED COMPANY PRESIDENTS IN 1970 BY SALARY AND OTHER PAYMENTS

Company	1970 Salary	Other Payments	Average Annual Dollar Value of Options Exercised
Xerox Corp. (C. Peter McColough)	$304,493	$ 64,546	$664,503 (1/66–3/71)
Chrysler Corp. (John J. Riccardo)	166,667	8,333	—
Ford Motor (Lee A. Iacocca)	200,000	264,999	174,054 (1/65–3/71)
Gneral Motors (Edward N. Cole)	225,000	11,250°°	—
IBM Corp. (T. Vincent Learson)	120,000	228,570	193,707 (1/66–2/71)
Chase Manhattan Corp. (Herbert P. Patterson)	160,000	24,000	—
First National City Corp. (William I. Spencer)	189,840	—	—
Boise Cascade Corp. (Robert V. Hansberger)	220,833	12,170	312,085 (1/65–2/70)
Georgia-Pacific (William H. Hunt)	130,040	13,040	36,853 (1/66–2/71)
Dow Chemical (Herbert D. Doan)	247,235	—	—
E. I. du Pont de Nemours (Charles B. McCoy)	193,000	173,655°°	—
W. R. Grace & Co. (J. Peter Grace)	285,000	—	—
Boeing Co. (Thornton A. Wilson)	139,848	5,594	—
Lockheed Aircraft (A. Carl Kotchian)	135,000	NA	NA
North American Rockwell (Robert Anderson)	218,833	—	—
American Telephone & Telegraph° (H. I. Romnes)	345,833	10,375°°	—
Columbia Broadcasting System (Frank Stanton)	200,000	196,450	—
International Telephone & Telegraph (Harold S. Geneen)	356,755	410,000	475,000 (1/65–3/71)
Honeywell, Inc. (Stephen F. Keating)	147,500	—	$198,500 (1/69–3/71)
Zenith Radio° (Joseph S. Wright)	110,000	52,564	85,821 (1/69–3/70)
Coca-Cola Co.° (J. Paul Austin)	183,333	50,000	—
Kraftco Corp. (William O. Beers)	220,816	—	2,880 (1/69–2/71)
PepsiCo Inc. (Donald M. Kendall)	150,000	51,400	204,438 (1/68–3/70)
Great Atlantic & Pacific Tea Co. (William J. Kane)	126,008	13,888	—
Aluminum Co. of America (W. H. Krome George)	157,000	50,442	1,050 (1/69–2/70)
Kaiser Aluminum & Chemical (T. J. Ready, Jr.)	335,000	—	23,118 (1/66–1/71)

Table 4 (continued)

Company	1970 Salary	Other Payments	Average Annual Dollar Value of Options Exercised
Corning Glass Works (R. Lee Waterman)	$135,000	$ 3,375	128,300 (1/66–1/71)
American Electric Power (Donald C. Cook)	231,785	16,376	—
Atlantic Richfield (Thornton F. Bradshaw)	300,872	6,000	665,300 (1/69–2/70)
Exxon Corp. (Milo M. Brisco)	212,500	117,750**	—
International Paper (Edward B. Hinman)	179,489	—	—
Johnson & Johnson (Richard B. Sellars)	211,917	135,718**	175,481 (1/66–2/71)
Pfizer, Inc.* (John J. Powers, Jr.)	250,025	—	26,456 (1/66–2/71)
New York Times (Arthur Ochs Sulzberger)	147,087	20,000	—
Sears, Roebuck & Co. (Arthur M. Wood)	275,000	1,740	210,594 (1/66–3/71)
Bristol-Myers (Richard L. Gelb)	165,000	119,843	—
Procter & Gamble (Howard J. Morgens)	425,000	61,025	—
United States Steel (Edgar B. Speer)	225,000	9,000	—
Firestone Tire & Rubber (Robert D. Thomas)	135,000	—	—
Trans World Airlines (Forwood C. Wiser, Jr.)	91,667	20,000	—

Note: The average annual dollar value of an option was arrived at by dividing the difference between what was paid and what was received for a stock by the number of years covered by the data. The period used to calculate the option is shown in parentheses below the average annual dollar figure.

*Indicates that the president is also chairman of the board.

**Denotes the fact that additional compensation was paid that is not included in either the salary or the "other payments" section.

Source: "For Top Executives: Huge Raises, Huge Cuts," *Business Week*, No. 2181 (June 19, 1971), 58–78.

Table 5

WHO OWNED THE NATION'S WEALTH IN 1967

Name	Source of Wealth	Age
$1–1.5 Billion		
J. Paul Getty	Getty Oil/Inheritor	75
Howard Hughes	Hughes Tool, Hughes Aircraft, etc.	62
$500 Million–$1 Billion		
H. L. Hunt	Oil	79
Dr. Edwin Land	Polaroid	58
Daniel K. Ludwig	Shipping	70
Ailsa Mellon Bruce	Rentier/Inheritor	66
Paul Mellon	Director, Mellon Bank/Inheritor	60
Richard King Mellon	Alcoa/Inheritor	68
$300–500 Million		
N. Bunker Hunt	Oil/Inheritor	42
John D. MacArthur	Insurance	71
William L. McKnight	Minnesota Mining and Manufacturing	80
Charles S. Mott	General Motors	92
R. E. (Bob) Smith	Oil, Real Estate	73
$200–300 Million		
Howard F. Ahmanson	Oil, Savings and Loan	61
Charles Allen, Jr.	Investment Banking	65
Mrs. W. Van Allen Clark, Sr. (Edna McConnell)	Avon Products/Inheritor	80
John T. Dorrance	Campbell Soup/Inheritor	49
Mrs. Alfred I. Du Pont	Company Director/Inheritor	84
Charles W. Engelhard, Jr.	Mining and Metal	51
Sherman M. Fairchild	Fairchild Camera/IBM	72
Leon Hess	Hess Oil and Chemical	54
William R. Hewlett	Hewlett-Packard	54
David Packard	Hewlett-Packard	55
Amory Houghton	Corning Glass/Inheritor	68
Joseph P. Kennedy	Market Operator	79
Eli Lilly	Eli Lilly & Company	83
Forrest E. Mars	Mars Candy	64
Samuel I. Newhouse	Newspapers	73
Marjorie Merriweather Post	General Foods/Inheritor	81
Mrs. Jean Mauze (Abby Rockefeller)	Rentier/Inheritor	64
David Rockefeller	Banker/Inheritor	52
John D. Rockefeller III	Inheritor	62
Laurance Rockefeller	Inheritor	57
Nelson Rockefeller	Governor/Inheritor	59

Table 5 (continued)

Name	Source of Wealth	Age
Winthrop Rockefeller	Governor/Inheritor	56
Cordelia Scaife May	Rentier/Inheritor	39
Richard Mellon Scaife	Rentier/Inheritor	35
DeWitt Wallace	*Reader's Digest*	78
Mrs. Charles Payson (Joan Whitney)	Inheritor	65
John Hay Whitney	Inheritor	63
$150–200 Million		
James S. Abercrombie	Oil/Iron	76
William Benton	*Encyclopaedia Britannica*	68
Jacob Blaustein	Standard Oil (Indiana)	75
Chester Carlson	Inventor of Xerography	62
Edward J. Daly	World Airways	45
Clarence Dillon	Banking	85
Doris Duke	Rentier/Inheritor	55
Lammot du Pont Copeland	Inheritor	62
Henry B. du Pont	Inheritor	69
Benson Ford	Ford/Inheritor	48
Mrs. W. Buhl Ford II (Josephine Ford)	Ford/Inheritor	44
William C. Ford	Ford/Inheritor	43
Helen Clay Frick	Steel/Inheritor	79
William T. Grant	Variety Stores	91
Bob Hope	Comedian	64
Arthur A. Houghton, Jr.	Corning Glass/Inheritor	61
J. Seward Johnson	Johnson & Johnson	72
Peter Kiewit	Construction	77
Allan P. Kirby	Inheritor	75
J. S. McDonnell, Jr.	Aircraft/Inheritor	69
Mrs. Lester J. Norris (Dellora F. Angell)	Inheritor	65
E. Claiborne Robins	Drugs	57
W. Clement Stone	Insurance	65
Mrs. Arthur Hays Sulzberger	Publishing/Inheritor	75
S. Mark Taper	First Financial Corp.	66
Robert W. Woodruff	Coca Cola/Inheritor	78

Source: "The Richest of the Rich," *Fortune* (May 1968), 156.

noteworthy exceptions, many of these fortunes are a direct
result of the war for wealth—that is, of the set of policies and
programs that provide special advantages to people who are
wise enough to invest their money in oil exploration, to export
wheat, to set up tax shelters, or to engage in any one of a
number of other government-subsidized activities.

THE TROUBLE WITH INCOME STATISTICS

The trouble with the income statistics published by the Census
Bureau is that they exclude several important sources of
income. As a result, these estimates have tended to be about
13 percent lower than those published by the Office of Business Economics. Since much of the excluded income is received
by those in the upper income brackets, the census data probably understate the true height of the income pyramid. The
key omissions are income in kind, realized capital gains, and
retained corporate earnings.

Income in kind is the income people receive in the form of
goods and services. A farmer may sell his crops and receive
income, or he and his family may consume them. If he sells
his crops, the income he receives enters into the census figures;
if he eats them, it does not. A housewife's services are not
counted in the census income data unless she hires herself out
as a maid. But these have a relatively small effect compared to
the income in kind provided by business.

Perhaps the best-known form of business income in kind is
the company expense account. Expense accounts are provided
to employees to reimburse them for out-of-pocket costs
incurred while conducting company business. The definition of
what constitutes a legitimate business cost has generally been
quite liberal, especially for top management. Private hunting
lodges, planes and yachts, hotel suites, and automobiles are
often provided to executives at company expense. And such
items of consumption as theater tickets and membership in
exclusive golf clubs and social clubs are frequently paid for by
the company and at least partially passed on to other taxpayers
at income tax time. In August 1957, an unofficial estimate
placed annual total expense account outlays at somewhere

between $5 billion and $10 billion, and the figure has probably increased several times over since then.[16] Because substantial expense accounts are usually available only to people with incomes over $15,000, the effect of excluding this form of income in kind from the income data is to understate the amount of income received by those higher up in the income distribution.

Several indirect forms of income in kind result from association with a large and prosperous company. A corporate executive usually finds it easier to borrow money at the local bank where his company has an account, and he may receive free checking-account services. He may also avail himself of the company's accountants' services and have access to its legal staff. If he is moving to a new location, his company may help in the search for a new home, provide special handling for the moving of his furniture, and guarantee the value of the property he puts up for sale. Unfortunately, it is not possible to put a price tag on services of this type because the data required to do so simply are not available. It seems clear, however, that if these services could be priced they would raise the average income of people in the upper brackets.

Several other forms of income in kind are also excluded from the census figures. A person who resides in his own home or condominium obtains an income in the form of consumer services. The homeowner is an investor who chooses to take his return in the form of services. To see this clearly, suppose that a homeowner decided to convert his income in kind into real income. He might do so by simply moving out of his house and renting it to someone else. The total amount of imputed rent in the United States is substantial. The U.S. Department of Commerce estimates that the American public received some $12.1 billion in imputed rent on owner-occupied housing in 1968. And since the dollar value of owned housing rises with income, it seems likely that those above the threshold of affluence receive greater income in kind from housing than those below it.

Other forms of imputed income that might legitimately be

[16] V. *Henry Rothschild and Rudolf Soberheim, "Expense Accounts for Executives,"* Yale Law Journal, 67 *(July 1958), 1363–1392.*

included in a definition of income are nonmoney wages, nonmoney farm income, imputed interest from financial inter-
mediaries, employer payments to welfare and pension funds,
and the services individuals receive from insurance companies
without having to pay for them. It seems reasonable to assume
that these raise the middle and upper ends of the income
distribution.

Table 4 provides a good illustration of how exclusion of
capital gains understates true income. In the case of the presidents of Xerox Corp., Boise Cascade Corp., International Telephone & Telegraph, IBM Corp., Honeywell, Inc., PepsiCo Inc.,
and Atlantic Richfield, the income figures reported to the
Census Bureau are less than half the true figure. And the presidents of Georgia-Pacific, William H. Hunt, Zenith Radio,
Corning Glass Works, Ford Motor, Johnson & Johnson, and
Sears, Roebuck & Co. actually had incomes at least 25 percent
greater than the figures likely to have been reported to the
Census Bureau. Moreover, the Census Bureau figures are
further understated because they do not include stock bonuses
and other nonmonetary compensation included in the "other
payments" column of Table 4.

What are the combined effects of all of these exclusions on
the income distribution statistics? In a paper delivered in 1971,
two members of the Census Bureau, Herman Miller and Roger
Herriott, tried to answer this question.[17] Using figures that
allow both for underreporting of income and for exclusions in
the census data, they confirmed the fact that Census Bureau
data understate the total number of families with incomes of
$50,000 or more. This conclusion is consistent with the IRS
data discussed earlier, but it fails to highlight the inequalities
of income within the $50,000-and-over group.

Figure 4 shows the relationship between the percentage of
total money income held by those at each income level and
the percentage of consumer units at that level. Notice what
happens to the lowest and highest income groups as a result
of the broader definition of income used by Herriott and

---

[17] *Roger Herriott and Herman Miller, "Who Paid the Taxes in
1968?" Paper prepared for the National Industrial Conference Board
meeting, New York City, March 18, 1971.*

Figure 4

COMPARISON OF CONSUMER UNITS AND MONEY INCOME
USING TWO DEFINITIONS OF INCOME, 1968

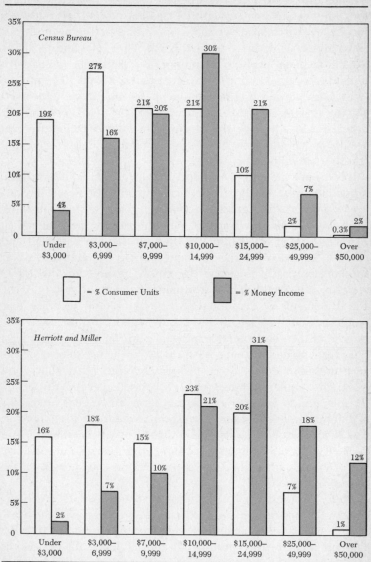

Source: Roger Herriott and Herman Miller, "Who Paid the Taxes in 1968?" Paper prepared for the National Industrial Conference Board meeting, New York, N.Y., March 18, 1971, p. 15.

Miller. Fewer consumer units have incomes of less than
$3,000, and those units remaining in this group after the data
are adjusted receive a slightly smaller portion of the total
income. Fewer consumer units are found at the second and
third levels, while more enter the $10,000–15,000 and $15,000–
24,000 income levels. The number of consumer units with
incomes of $15,000 or more increases by about 10.1 million,
or 16 percent, and the percentage of the total income received
by this group increases from 31 percent to 61 percent. In
other words, adjusting the census data for the excluded items
results in an increase in the percentage of units above the
threshold of affluence.

This is not the end of the story, however. The effect of these
adjustments on the top of the income distribution may be seen
by examining the figures for the top 1 percent of consumer
units. By the Census Bureau's definition, consumer units with
incomes of over $32,000 in 1968 fall into the top 1 percent and
receive 5 percent of the total income. If the Herriott-Miller
measure is used, however, the cutoff income for the top 1
percent is $60,000. Those fortunate enough to fall into the
top 1 percent receive about 9 percent of total income. This
suggests that the Census Bureau data tend to understate the
degree of income inequality prevalent in the United States.

Several objections have been raised to the use of single-year
measures of income. Some economists argue that short-term
transitory and/or random changes exaggerate the dispersion
of incomes if income is estimated on an annual basis. To
obtain a superior measure, they propose that researchers average income over a longer period. Yet recent panel studies of
income collected over several consecutive years do not confirm
the existence of a substantial upward bias arising from the
use of annual data.[18]

Some economists also point out that annual data are sensi-
tive to the business cycle. Profits fluctuate more over the cycle
than does national income. People receiving a large portion
of their income from profits will end up lower in the income

[18] *U.S. Congress, Joint Economic Committee,* The Distribution of Personal Income (*Washington, D.C.: U.S. Government Printing Office, 1965*),
p. 27.

distribution during recessions than in times of prosperity. And since this group is more concentrated in the upper income groups, there is a tendency for incomes to become more unequal in good times. Interestingly, however, another phenomenon works in the opposite direction. In bad times the least productive workers are the first to lose their jobs, while skilled workers and managers remain employed. With a surplus of unskilled workers on the market, the wage differential between unskilled and skilled workers widens and is reflected in a more unequal income distribution. Prosperity brings both greater employment opportunities and higher wages to the unskilled. The rise in the income of the unskilled tends to overshadow the rise in the incomes of the wealthy induced by corporate profits so that, on the whole, incomes tend to become more equal during periods of prosperity.

A third objection to a single-year measure is that annual income data do not reflect an individual's lifetime potential. Some economists have proposed the construction of lifetime income profiles as a basis for measuring the distribution of income. They argue that information on an individual's income at a certain point in time indicates neither what he has already received nor what he will receive in the future. Since annual estimates of income are related to both the age and the education of the population, a single-year measure underestimates the equality of incomes in a society with young, highly educated workers. There is a real question, however, as to how to measure a person's lifetime income. Estimates of lifetime earnings constructed from data collected at one point in time can be quite controversial. For example, economists are likely to disagree on the population to include in the lifetime distributions, the way to discount the benefits received in future years, the assumptions to be made regarding the potential for employment, and the growth rate to be applied in projecting future changes.

INCOME INEQUALITY OVER TIME

Despite the problems posed by the use of money income data, many social scientists have used data supplied by the Census

Bureau and the *Survey of Consumer Finance* to determine whether the income distribution is becoming more or less equal over time. From the publication of Simon Kuznet's famous study *Shares of Upper Income Groups in Income and Saving* until the early 1960s, it was fashionable to agree, as the National Bureau of Economic Research did in a 1951 press release, that the "United States has travelled a considerable distance toward absolute equality of incomes." More recently this view has given way to the realization that the income distribution has not changed significantly since 1947, at least if available income figures are any guide.

What has been happening to the shares of pretax personal income held by families? To answer this question we shall divide all of the families in the United States into ten groups of equal size. This enables us to analyze how much of the national income went to the top and bottom tenths in each of several time periods. The data are shown in Figure 5. Notice that the share of income going to the highest tenth has been fairly constant in the long run but has risen by about 2 percent since 1960. On the other hand, the income share of those in the lowest tenth has fallen over the long run and has remained relatively constant during the past eight years. A different conclusion would be reached if data from the Census Bureau were used. But some experts question the validity of those data.

If any consensus exists at all, it is probably summed up in the following comment by Professor Eugene Smolensky, a noted economic historian:

It is the judgment of most experts in this area that the data are biased toward overestimating the degree of decline in income inequality. This judgment rests . . . on the belief that capital gains and income supplements in the form of expense accounts, automobiles, stock options, etc., are accruing to a much greater extent at the upper end of the income distribution than at the lower, and these do not find their way into the income-distribution statistics. A bias of less than one half of 1 percent in the income share would be sufficient to wipe out all the gains made by the lowest quartiles since 1935.[19]

So much for the growing equality of income in the United States!

[19] *Eugene Smolensky, "The Past and Present Poor," in Stanley Engerman (ed.),* A Reinterpretation of American History *(New York: Harper & Row, Publishers, Inc., 1971), pp. 95–96.*

Figure 5

PERCENTAGE OF NATIONAL PERSONAL INCOME BEFORE TAXES RECEIVED BY HIGHEST, SECOND-HIGHEST, AND BOTTOM INCOME TENTHS *(Selected Years)*

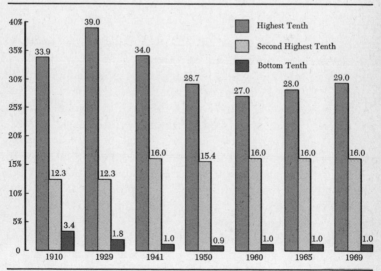

Source: For 1910–1950, Gabriel Kolko, *Wealth and Power in America* (New York: Praeger Publishers, Inc., 1962), p. 14; for 1960 and 1965, George Katona, *1968 Survey of Consumer Finances* (Ann Arbor, Mich.: Braum-Brumfield, 1969), p. 19; 1969 data from *1970 Survey of Consumer Finances* (Ann Arbor, Mich.: Braum-Brumfield, 1970), p. 9.

3
WHO
SHALL INHERIT
THE EARTH

*Now the universal ideal of capitalism is that
man, being created a little lower than
the angels, should raise himself to their
level in this respect by the acquisition
of property . . .*
—SIDNEY OLIVER

Accumulation of wealth is not inevitable. Through an effective system of death taxes, society can limit the wealth transferred from one generation to another. The total amount of privately held wealth in America probably exceeds $2.5 trillion. If this wealth changed hands once every 30 years, about $83 billion would be available for taxation each year. However, the annual death tax receipts collected by the federal and state governments total only $5 billion, slightly less than 6 percent of the total annual wealth accumulated by families. Thus it would appear that our present tax system does little to prevent the transfer of wealth from one generation to another.

Death taxes can be a useful tool in the implementation of policies designed to limit the concentration of wealth. By taxing property accumulations away after the person who earned them (or his spouse) dies, a society can limit the concentration of property over time. It can also use the tax receipts to reduce the taxes paid by the poor. Despite the obvious benefit to society, few governments have chosen to adopt death tax policies that take a strong bite out of the fortunes of the rich. This is no accident. An effective set of policies would be costly to the warriors for wealth.

In evaluating the existing tax structures we shall consider

several issues: First, to what extent are property rights essential to ensure the smooth operation of a market economy? Second, what are the pros and cons of death taxation? Third, how is it that estate tax rates—equal to about 77 percent on fortunes of $10 million or more—have so little effect on the concentration of wealth in the United States? Finally, what effects would a strong antiaccumulation policy have on the operation of the economy?

DEATH AND PERPETUAL SOVEREIGNTY

Despite the pronouncements of the more conservative elements of our society, property rights were not handed to mankind on a stone tablet. These rights have been (and are) culturally determined and have changed along with the institutions they protect. In ancient times property was transferred between generations in such a natural manner that inheritance laws were unnecessary. Land title was often granted directly to a family; where the state did not grant formal recognition of ownership, occupancy was often a sufficient condition to obtain a property right. Families were usually of an extended nature so that a man and his wife, children, grandchildren, and distant relatives all lived together, sharing possessions and a way of life. A family collectively tilled the soil, harvested the crops, and defended the property against external threats. "Togetherness" was more than a slogan—it grew out of the agricultural way of life.

In this type of society the death of the head of a household had little effect on property ownership. Inheritance was a right that one earned by participating in family activities. This assumption is implicit in ancient thought, as may be seen in this passage from *The Libation Bearers*, in which Orestes says to Zeus: "I, with my sister, whom I name, Electra, here stand in your sight, children whose father is lost. We both are driven from a house that should be ours. If you destroy these fledglings of a father who gave you sacrifice and high honor, from what hand like his shall you be given the sacred feast which is your right?"

Times have changed, and so has the nature of property

ownership. Families no longer live together in large groups, and property is shared in common less often. Today's family is nuclear; relatively few pieces of property are jointly owned. Children have their "own" rooms, parents "own" separate cars, and members of the family may have their "own" tennis rackets, golf clubs, and savings accounts. When one family member gives property to another, it is usually at his pleasure and not necessarily because the other has earned it. This phenomenon, referred to earlier as privatization, has affected not only the way in which wealth is displayed but also the patterns of ownership in our society and the right of a property owner to bequeath his goods.

Throughout history the many generations of warriors for wealth have worked to shape the direction and scope of the inheritance laws. Biblical patriarchs sought perpetual sovereignty for their houses through the use of primogeniture laws. Recall, for example, the animosity between Cain and Abel, and the jealousy of Joseph's brothers. During the Dark Ages the clergy maintained their sovereignty through the powers of appointment given under ecclesiastical law. And as the notion of royalty developed, so did the doctrine of divine right, which was designed to give monarchs the right to bequeath entire kingdoms to their heirs.

The onset of the industrial revolution and the rising belief in an individualistic ethic were fair game for the new warriors. As Le Tourneau wrote in 1896, "The palm is not offered to the best—that is, to the individuals most endowed with intelligence and character—but to those who, in one way or another, and even by skillfully maneuvering between certain awkward clauses of the law, succeed in amassing great fortunes."[1]

PROPERTY LAWS AND THE ECONOMIC SYSTEM

Many of the property laws that currently govern our economic system are written in a language reflecting the commercial needs of the time. Without these laws free exchange

[1] *Charles Le Tourneau,* Property: Its Origin and Development *(New York: Charles Scribner's Sons, 1896), p. 378.*

would not be possible and the great industrial marketplaces of the western world could not exist. But precisely because these laws are commercially inspired, the protection they grant is remarkably limited. No nation acknowledges the inherent right of citizens to privacy, quiet, or clean air. Nor does any nation recognize the right of future generations to live in an uncrowded world. Although some aspects of tax law cover the problems of privacy and quiet, they fail to deal with a host of infringements on privacy ranging from transistor radios and dune buggies on public beaches to the problem of jet noise. Our property laws are tailored to the imperatives of the economic system and to an individualistic society. Large companies, and to a lesser extent single individuals, are free to use their property in a manner that may impose substantial external costs on others.

Unrestricted Bequests

While the right to claim title to property is a necessary condition for the operation of an exchange economy, it is not a sufficient reason for permitting unrestricted bequests. In a market economy individuals must be free to exchange property while they are alive: The economy would probably continue to operate smoothly if property ownership terminated at death. Several legal scholars have argued that ownership is not complete unless a thing can be bestowed at the owner's pleasure. By this definition few societies grant "complete" property rights.

Every society places some restrictions on the ownership of property. The United States does not permit its citizens to possess hand grenades, to grow marijuana, or to purchase or sell gold in foreign markets. Most societies reserve the right to restrict property rights when the exercise of these rights interferes with the public interest.

A second justification for unrestricted bequests is the principle of consumer sovereignty, which states that the consumer should receive the goods for which he is willing to pay. If the consumer is truly sovereign, by what right can we deny him the opportunity to dispense with his estate as he sees fit? What is the difference between allowing him to purchase an insurance policy that will provide funds to his heirs after he is dead and permitting him to bequeath his fortune directly to his heirs? If the consumer is free to spend his money as he sees fit, why shouldn't he be free to save it for the future use of others?

Two issues are actually at stake. One involves the consumer's right to dispose of his property as he sees fit. The other involves the question of whether consumers should be permitted to exercise perpetual sovereignty over the economic system. Existing inheritance laws permit the preferences of the deceased to control the resources of future generations. A man who creates a foundation with his wealth, for example, can ensure that the resources of future generations will be channeled into medicine, education, business, or any other area of his choice. Moreover, by passing his money to his heirs in a form that avoids future taxation, he also affects the taxable income base of future generations. And a man who places his estate in trust can specify who receives the principal and interest, when it will be paid, and the conditions governing its eventual use.

A family's control over a company can be maintained over many years through the use of foundations and holding companies. The Ford Foundation, for example, is likely to keep a Ford in our lives for many years to come. As Ferdinand Lundberg puts it,

> By converting all its remaining Class A stock into voting stock the foundation could dilute the voting power of the presently outstanding common to 30 percent of the present capital structure. With the 30 percent of the voting power in the newly converted common plus the 40 percent of voting power in Class B stock the Fords would actually have, as they now potentially have, 70 percent of the voting power.[2]

Likewise, the remarkable interrelationship between E. I. du Pont de Nemours and Christiana Securities, a $2.2-billion

[2] *Ferdinand Lundberg,* The Rich *and the* Super Rich *(New York: Bantam Books, Inc., 1969), p. 194.*

financial holding company, links the Du Pont family closely to the management of the huge chemical company. For example, Irénée Du Pont, Jr., is president of Christiana and holds approximately $27 million of its stock; he is also a director of the chemical company and owns $1.5 million of its stock. Lammot du Pont Copeland is vice president of Christiana and holds $14 million of its stock; he is currently a director of Du Pont (formerly its chairman of the board) and owns $35 million of Du Pont stock. And according to *The New York Times*, five directors of Du Pont serve as directors of Christiana, while seven additional Du Pont directors own shares of Christiana common.[3] The extensive holdings of Du Pont stock controlled by the Du Pont family through Christiana Securities help make the chemical company a family business.

Family trusts do not provide the same opportunities for control as foundations and holding companies, although they offer unique powers to the few large banks that administer them. These banks manage large sums of money and stock, and are thus in a position to affect the policies of the leading corporations. They almost always encourage conservative approaches to management. A recent nationwide study by a congressional committee headed by Representative Wright Patman found, for example, that only 49 banks held $135.2 billion in trust assets, or 54 percent of the total trust assets covered by the study. The committee also found substantial evidence of interlocking directorships between these banks and the top 500 corporations. Defenders of the banking industry claim that such directorships are necessary to ensure the safety of their clients' funds. Nonetheless, the committee argued that most big businessmen are aware of the influence big banks exert over their production decisions.[4]

While the principle of consumer sovereignty may be used to justify a man's right to dispose of his property as he wishes, it does not necessarily require acceptance of the idea of per-

---

[3] The New York Times, *November 23, 1972, p. 55.*
[4] *U.S. Congress, House Committee on Banking and Currency,* Commercial Banks and Their Trust Activities: Emerging Influences on the American Economy *(Washington, D.C.: U.S. Government Printing Office, July 1968), pp. 13–16.*

petual sovereignty. An economic system should serve its participants. There is no *a priori* reason for it to serve the wishes of people who are dead and buried. The desire to leave an inheritance to one's family may provide an important work incentive, however; we shall return to this point shortly.

DEATH TAXES AND THE WARRIORS FOR WEALTH

Two basic types of death taxes are currently in existence, one called the estate tax and the other referred to as the inheritance tax. The former tax is levied on the estate left by a decedent; the latter is placed on the value of an estate after it has been transferred to the beneficiary. Estate taxes date back to Roman times. Adam Smith, writing in 1776, takes note of the Vicesima Hereditatum, "the twentieth penny of inheritance." This was a tax imposed by Augustus on the transference of property from the dead to the living.[5] Inheritance taxes came into fashion during the Middle Ages. If the deceased left no direct heirs, his property would revert to the crown. More distant relatives could acquire title to the property, however, by agreeing to pay a "relief" to the crown.

The unrestricted transfer of property from one generation to another has been favored by wealth warriors for many years, although an occasional warrior has broken from the ranks. No less eminent a man than Andrew Carnegie argued that bequests spoil the child and ruin the incentives built into a free-enterprise system. In *The Gospel of Wealth* he wrote, "The parent who leaves his son enormous wealth generally deadens the talents and energies of the son and tempts him to lead a less useful and less worthy life than he otherwise would."[6] Other eminent men publicly opposed to liberal inheritance laws were Theodore and Franklin Roosevelt and Herbert Hoover. The argument against inheritances is usually stated as follows: A person's income represents a potential claim on society's resources. It is also a reward for the services

[5] *Adam Smith,* The Wealth of Nations *(New York: Modern Library, Inc., 1937),* p. 811.
[6] *Andrew Carnegie in Edward C. Kirkland (ed.),* The Gospel of Wealth *(Cambridge, Mass.: Harvard University Press, 1962),* p. 50.

he contributes to the economic system. Inheritances are transfers of assets (representing potential income) from the people who earned them to people who did not. To maintain the incentives necessary for the operation of the economy society should tax away unearned rewards.

Opponents of death taxation question these arguments, and their viewpoint seems to dominate public attitudes. According to Joseph A. Pechman, an expert on federal taxes, "The average family in the United States still aspires to improved economic and social status, and the estate and gift taxes are erroneously regarded as especially burdensome to the family that is beginning to prosper through hard work and saving."[7] Pechman suggests that some people dislike the estate tax because it includes such items as the family home and car, series E bonds, and savings bank deposits; for the uninitiated these items do not seem to be forms of wealth.

It is especially ironic that the common man resents death taxes. Those who pay estate taxes are a very small and elite percentage of the population. In 1966, for example, only 97,000 estate tax forms were filed. This is primarily a result of a congressional decision to exempt the first $60,000 of a person's estate from taxation. A person's gross estate consists of all the property in his possession at the time of death. It also includes gifts made within three years of death, insurance, and the value of any trusts that the person was free to revoke. Trusts that are irrevocable escape taxation, as we shall see.

The federal tax rates are quite mild at the low end of the scale. A person with a gross estate of $64,000 is taxed at a rate of only 3 percent on the value of his estate in excess of $60,000 —that is, $120 in taxes—unless he takes advantage of other provisions of the law. A person whose estate has a net value of $10 million or more is taxed at a rate of 77 percent on the value of the estate in excess of $10 million. On paper, the estate tax is progressive—that is, the tax rate levied on the estate rises with the value of the estate. In practice, the laws are filled with loopholes that reduce the progressiveness of the

---

[7] *Joseph A. Pechman*, Federal Tax Policy *(New York: W. W. Norton & Company, Inc., 1971), p. 187.*

tax and provide a ready market for the employment of resourceful lawyers and accountants. If one is rich and/or knowledgeable, his family wealth can be kept intact. Examples follow.

Charity Begins in the Home

A well-advised property owner bequeaths half his wealth to his wife. This simple act temporarily places a portion of his estate beyond taxation at the time of his death. Although the portion he gives to his wife will be taxed when she dies, the rates applied to the total estate will be lower. To see how this works, consider the following example: Suppose that Mr. Vandafeller owns property worth $1 million and bequeaths half to his wife and half to his children. Without this bequest his gross estate before taxation would be $1 million, and his taxable estate, after deducting $60,000, would be $940,000. Because the law permits a marital deduction, Vandafeller can give half his property to his wife, thereby reducing his gross estate to $500,000 and his taxable estate to $440,000.

The marital deduction favors the very rich. This is because the amount of the tax deduction increases as one's estate increases. If Mr. Vandafeller leaves a gross estate of $1 million, roughly $500,000 can be excluded from the estate as his wife's share. If he leaves a gross estate of $2 million, the amount increases to roughly $1 million. Although the excluded amount is eventually subject to taxation when the spouse dies, the marital deduction decreases the tax rate on the estate. The effective tax rate on a gross estate of $1 million is about 30 percent, ignoring the effects of the marital deduction.[8] If Vandafeller leaves half his estate to his wife, however, the average tax rate levied on both halves of the estate is only about 27 percent. The net tax saving from splitting the estate is about $30,000. Similarly, for a taxable estate of $10 million the effective tax rate is about 61 percent and the estate saves almost $1.2 million over the statutory rate through the marital deduction.

Another effect of the marital deduction is that it gives Mrs.

[8] *Pechman, p. 266.*

Vandafeller the use of half the estate, tax free. If she invests her $500,000 in tax-free municipals at a 5 percent interest rate, at the end of 10 years her estate will be worth $815,000. Had her half been taxed at the 25 percent rate before she received it, the $500,000 would have been worth $375,000 after taxes. In 10 years this amount would have grown to only $611,000 at the 5 percent interest rate. Postponing taxation of her portion of the estate has an obvious monetary advantage equal to $204,000.

Several changes in the existing law have been recommended. Some experts suggest including inheritances in the recipient's taxable income: Inheritances are then subject to federal income taxation. Others suggest treating husband and wife as a single unit. A separate tax is then levied on their combined estates and paid in installments, the first at the death of one spouse and the second after the death of the remaining spouse. But thus far Congress has shown little interest in enacting either type of reform.

The Great Giveaway

It pays to be generous. An estate can be passed from one generation to the next far more easily if it is given away—preferably over a long period. Suppose that Harry Thomas offers a yearly sum to his brother Homer. Under the gift tax laws Harry's offering will be taxed only if it is greater than $3,000 and if Harry has given Homer gifts of more than $30,000 in the past. If Harry is married, Homer can receive up to $6,000 each year, and Homer's lifetime gift exemption increases to 60,000. Since there is no limit on the number of people to whom Harry can give money, a substantial amount of his estate may be transferred tax free before he dies.

Gift giving enables wealthy families to pay a lower estate tax than they otherwise might. Several factors are involved. First, by giving a portion of his estate away while he is alive a person can decrease the rate at which the government taxes his property: The portion of his estate that is given away is subject to the gift tax, and the remainder comes under the estate tax. Each of these taxes is progressive, so the tax rate depends on the value of the gifts (for the gift tax) and that of the estate (for the estate tax). Because the transfer of property takes place under two taxes, the tax rates applied in each case are lower than if the entire estate were taxed at once. Second, gift tax rates are 25 percent lower than estate tax rates. An estate taxed at a 28 percent rate under the estate tax is taxed at 21 percent under the gift tax. Third, certain technicalities make the amount included in the gift tax base smaller than the amount included in the estate tax base. (The tax base is the monetary amount on which the tax rate is levied.) Finally, because of various gift tax exemptions and exclusions, large gifts can be given to family members tax free, especially if such gifts are made annually.

The advantages of the gift tax, as opposed to the estate tax, become quite important in the higher income brackets. If Mr. Aurelia gives his son gifts worth $5 million during his lifetime, he pays a gift tax of "only" $1.8 million. To leave the same $5 million at the time of his death, Aurelia must accumulate a $15 million estate, and his estate must pay $10 million in estate taxes. The same gift costs $8.2 million more after his death!

The rich transfer a small percentage of their estates, but the total sums involved are quite substantial. In a study of 1957 and 1959 gift tax returns, it was found that only 29 percent of the decedents with estates involving gross property transfers under $900,000 filed gift tax returns. About 54 percent of the 2,256 millionaire decedents made taxable gifts in the period between 1932 and the time of death. And at the highest wealth levels (millionaire decedents with gross transfers of $10 million or more), 50 out of the 52 decedents reported some gift giving! The total value of the gifts reported by this group, including gifts to charity, came to only 14 percent of the total value of the property transferred after death; nonetheless, the amount transferred was $1.11 billion![9] Note that in Figure 6 the total amount transferred in gifts generally rises with the gross value of the estate.

Why don't wealthy people transfer larger portions of their estates while they are alive—in other words, why aren't more

[9] *Carl Shoup*, Federal Estate and Gift Taxes (*Washington, D.C.: The Brookings Institution, 1966*), *pp. 18–31.*

Figure 6

NONCHARITABLE LIFETIME GIFTS BY SIZE OF ESTATE IN 1959

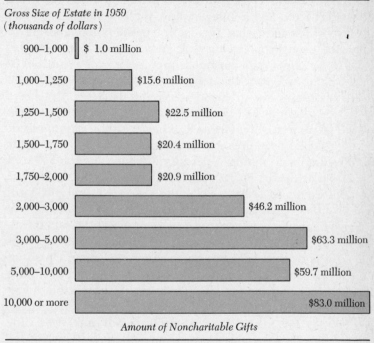

Gross Size of Estate in 1959
(thousands of dollars)

900–1,000	$ 1.0 million
1,000–1,250	$15.6 million
1,250–1,500	$22.5 million
1,500–1,750	$20.4 million
1,750–2,000	$20.9 million
2,000–3,000	$46.2 million
3,000–5,000	$63.3 million
5,000–10,000	$59.7 million
10,000 or more	$83.0 million

Amount of Noncharitable Gifts

Source: Carl Shoup, *Federal Estate and Gift Taxes* (Washington, D.C.: The Brookings Institution, 1966), p. 40.

gifts made *inter vivos?* Several things must be considered: First, many people prefer to avoid thinking about death. Since the timing of death is uncertain, the elderly try to keep large sums available to cover medical expenses and other personal needs. Thus they are unwilling to part with their funds even if it means a smaller bequest to their heirs. Second, as one author puts it, "The rich probably do believe that money is power, and while *inter vivos* transfer of money is often agreeable to the donor, no one who has tasted power yields it without reluctance."[10] A man's estate often provides him with

[10] *Shoup, p. 21.*

a source of control over both his business enterprises and his family. Third, bequestors may hold back on property transfers to avoid spoiling their children. Also, they may be concerned with maintaining control of their wealth in order to avoid dependency on others. Interestingly, the comments of several tax experts suggest that the latter consideration appears to influence even people with very large wealth holdings. This leads to an important postulate of the war for wealth: For public policy to benefit the rich, it must recognize their inherent needs of certainty, control, and power.

Several alternatives have been suggested to limit the extent of the great giveaway. One is to integrate the estate and gift taxes. Under this proposal the government would levy a tax on all gifts made during a person's lifetime plus the value of his estate at death. The tax is cumulative, and the yearly and lifetime exemptions available under the estate and gift taxes can be either combined (as the Treasury suggested in 1969) or removed entirely. Under the Treasury proposal the rate schedule would be roughly 20 percent less than the present estate tax rates and would rise progressively with income. Husbands and wives could transfer funds to each other freely, but transfers to other members of the family would be taxable under the integrated tax. Another alternative is to tax inheritances through the existing income tax. For husbands and wives filing joint returns, this avoids taxing common property while the spouse is alive. At the spouse's death the property is treated as income for the recipients of the estate—it is taxed at federal income tax rates. Gifts are also counted as part of a person's income. A third suggestion is to enact an accessions tax. This is a progressive tax on a person's total acquisitions from gifts and inheritances. Each time a person receives a gift, he recalculates his tax and subtracts it from what he has already paid to the government. The difference is a gift to Uncle Sam.

In Trust for . . .

Trusts originated as a device for avoiding the law. In thirteenth-century England the Statutes of Mortmain prohibited individuals from transferring property to the church. Since a donor could transfer property to someone legally able to own it, land was transferred to a recipient with instructions to utilize it for the benefit of the church. Although the English courts of common law originally refused to uphold such use of property, the courts of chancery directed that the terms of transfer be followed and that the income from the property be conveyed to the church. If the owner of the property refused to follow the directions of the transferor, the church could sue for relief in the courts of chancery.

The modern version of the trust may also be used to circumvent the law. A favorite device for doing so is called generation skipping. Mr. Mustang, a wealthy doctor, leaves $3 million in the hands of a trustee (usually a banker, lawyer, or family friend). Under the terms of his trust agreement, Mustang's children are to receive any income earned from the $3 million during their lifetime. When they die, the $3 million (plus or minus any change in the value of capital) will be turned over to Mustang's grandchildren. An estate tax is paid when Mustang dies and again when his grandchildren die; his children pay no estate tax. Although Mustang's children enjoy the use of the property, it is not theirs, and under the terms of the law they need not pay an estate tax. Property placed in this type of trust skips taxes for one generation.

Generation skipping reduces the base on which the estate tax can be levied, thus reducing the bite of the tax. Suppose, for example, that all people with net estates of over $60,000 left their property in trusts that skipped one generation. Suppose, too, that the estate tax base is constant and that all of the generations live for the same length of time. Viewing the tax base over several generations, we find that half of the tax base is lost: Generation one pays the tax and two avoids it, three pays and four skips, and so on.

But this is not the greatest possible loss. Trusts can be established that avoid taxes for *more* than one generation. If the wealthy place their property in trusts skipping two generations, the estate tax base is reduced to one-third, and a three-generation trust reduces the base to one-fourth of its original size. The tax base continues to diminish as the number of generations included in the trust agreement increases. Fortunately, however, most states restrict the length of time over which trusts can extend, and under present restrictions the number of generations that can be skipped is usually three.

The impact of generation skipping can be enormous. Joseph Ruskay and Richard Osserman, in *Halfway to Tax Reform,* cite the case of William Randolph Hearst, Sr., the so-called Lord of San Simeon. Hearst left a fortune worth hundreds of millions at the time of his death. His estate paid a substantial estate tax in 1951 but because of the use of generation-skipping trusts it is unlikely to pay another tax until 2050 or later. By then it should be worth several billion dollars.[11]

The wealthy have been quick to recognize the attractiveness of generation-skipping trusts. The study cited above found that among estates valued at less than $300,000 in 1949 about 44 percent of the total value of the estates skipped taxes for one generation; the percentage increased to 65 percent of the value of the estates of $1 million or more. Moreover, the percentage of total millionaire estates creating trusts increased significantly with the size of the estate, as shown in Figure 7. In 1959, for example, 52 percent of the gross estates worth $1.00–1.25 million created trusts; the percentage rose to 77 percent for gross estates worth $10 million or more.[12]

If concentrations of wealth are to be limited, something must be done about generation-skipping trusts. Several alternative policies are available:

1. Treat trusts as if the property generating the income belonged to the recipient of the income. An estate tax would then be levied on the sum of the value of the recipient's nontrust property plus the value of the property held in trust. This practice is currently followed by the British.
2. Impose a new tax on the value of property held in trust. Graduated tax rates would be imposed according to the size of the trust, and rates lower than those of the estate tax would be chosen in recognition of the fact that the income recipient does not have complete freedom to manage his property.
3. Impose a separate tax on the property recipient when the trust dissolves.
4. Tax trust property but only after the first generation. This is the solution favored by many tax accountants.

[11] *Joseph Ruskay and Richard Osserman,* Halfway to Tax Reform *(Bloomington: University of Indiana Press, 1970), pp. 145–146.*
[12] *Shoup, pp. 40, 156, 161.*

Figure 7

DOLLAR AMOUNT OF TRUST BEFORE TAXES—1959

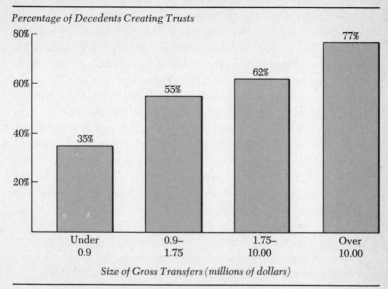

Percentage of Decedents Creating Trusts

Source: Carl Shoup, *Federal Estate and Gift Taxes* (Washington, D.C.: The Brookings Institution, 1966), pp. 40, 156, 161.

Whose Life Should You Insure?

Life insurance provides a nest egg to tide a man's family over after he dies. Since 1954 it has also become an effective way of passing funds from one generation to another without paying taxes. How does this work? There are several methods, but we shall present only one to illustrate the process. Mr. and Mrs. Cartweal buy a "fully-paid-at-65" life insurance policy for their eleven-year-old grandchild. They pay a premium of $6,000 a year for four years. (This premium is equal to the annual amount allowable under the gift tax.) At the end of the fourth year and thereafter, a $6,000 premium is automatically borrowed from the cash value of the life insurance policy.

Although an interest charge (usually 6 percent) is levied by the company, it can be deducted from the policy owner's income tax. And the value of the insurance policy begins to grow. A policy purchased for their grandchild at age 11 has substantial value when he dies. If he should die at age 25, for example, his estate would receive $492,549, at age 30, over $520,000. Despite the borrowings to pay premiums, by age 30 the policy has a *cash* value of almost $54,000. This might be used by the grandchild to purchase a new home, open a professional practice, or start a new business.

A life insurance policy bought for a grandchild is transferred between generations without a penny of estate tax. But if Cartweal purchases a policy of equal value on his own life, the value of the policy is included in his estate and taxed at the time of his death. Of course, Cartweal could transfer the ownership of his life insurance to his wife or children. If this transfer takes place more than three years before his death, the proceeds may not be included in his estate, even though he has paid all the premiums on the insurance.

Life insurance payments of the type just described were included in the estate tax base before 1954. This fact did not go unrecognized by the warriors for wealth, who argued that this inclusion made the estate tax "inequitable." "Since other forms of property given to an heir are not taxed," they argued, "why should insurance be discriminated against?" The argument worked so well that we find it now being used to oppose taxes on first-generation trusts. Spokesmen for the trusts argue that a tax on trusts would discriminate against them and in favor of life insurance. This pattern of using one special privilege in defense of another, called the *pyramid effect*, will become more obvious when we discuss the tax laws in chapters 6 and 7.

From the Left Pocket to the Right One

One practice of the Internal Revenue Service (IRS) is particularly bizarre—that of letting a taxpayer use discount bonds that are redeemable at par value to pay estate taxes. Those in the know refer to bonds of this type as "flower" bonds. To understand how flower bonds are used, consider the following example: Mr. Right, an octogenarian of the warlord class, purchases 100 flower bonds—worth $1,000 apiece when they mature in February 1980—for $860 per bond. Shortly thereafter Right dies; his estate turns these bonds in to the IRS and receives a $100,000 credit against taxes, even though the bonds cost Right only $86,000.

Flower bonds have slightly lower yields than other securities. This has the effect of discouraging purchases by the average investor. Nonetheless, in 1971 *The New York Times* reported that these bonds were being used to pay estate taxes at a rate of $40–50 million a month![13] Although the Treasury no longer issues new flower bonds, over $17 billion worth of bonds are still outstanding and some can be purchased at substantial discounts. Flower bonds, like generation-skipping trusts and the gift tax, are rarely of any use to the ordinary citizen. But to the wealthy they represent yet another way in which accumulations of wealth can be maintained.

THE ECONOMIC EFFECTS OF DEATH TAXES

The last few sections have presented several examples of how the estate tax laws favor the rich. An abundance of tax-saving devices, as well as the staggering savings they provide, are a testament to the unsung generations of lawyers and accountants who worked to make these laws what they are today. Few other equity questions have been as well debated as those involving inheritance taxes on the incomes of the rich. And few have engendered such lasting concern for the equity of minority groups—the rich and the very rich.

If the corrective policies suggested in the preceding sections are followed, they may be accompanied by several economic effects. An inheritor might reduce the level of his consumption. This follows from the fact that, although the timing of his inheritance is uncertain, he can make a reasonable estimate of expected future income and adjust his consumption accordingly. A steeper inheritance tax will reduce his expected future income, causing him either to reduce his consumption or to work harder in order to maintain the previous level. In either event the overall effects of the tax can be offset by appropriate fiscal and monetary policies. For example, if a steeper inheritance

[13] The New York Times, *May 6, 1971.*

tax reduces consumption, the government can reduce income taxes, increase the money supply, or increase expenditures on social programs. Economic theory suggests that these actions will offset the demand-reducing effects of a rise in the inheritance tax. Similarly, if a rise in tax rates decreases investment, the government can take steps that will counteract the adverse effects on the economy.

Death taxes may also affect the behavior of the bequestor. Consider the possibilities: (1) The bequestor is concerned solely with the size of his estate while he is alive. In this case a more rigorous death tax is unlikely to affect his behavior. (2) The bequestor wishes to leave a specific sum to his children. He might then decide to work more or to consume less if a higher tax is imposed. (3) The amount left to his children is related to the amount the bequestor consumes himself. A high death tax might then cause him to consume more and save less. In cases (2) and (3) the effects of death taxes can be offset by policies like those discussed in the last paragraph. (4) The bequestor is working primarily to leave an inheritance to his children. This truly beneficent man is the one usually pointed to by opponents of death taxes. In the absence of a very steep death tax, his behavior should not be very different from that described in case (2).

Several other aggregate economic effects are worth noting. Revenues from higher death taxes can be used to reduce the taxes collected from other sources. Unfortunately such reductions are likely to be rather small. High death taxes may also increase the demand for cash balances. As indicated in Chapter 1, households allocate their wealth among different types of assets so as to balance their desire for income against liquidity needs. The estate tax requires that cash be available within a short time after the estate holder's death. In recognition of this fact, a household head may choose to hold more money than he or she otherwise might. A rise in the estate tax may thus lead to increased demand for money and reduced demand for bonds and other assets. This may cause interest rates to rise and national income to fall. Moreover, a high death tax may reduce total investment by channeling funds away from private savings and into the U.S. Treasury. Nonetheless, the negative effects of the tax can probably be offset by appropriate fiscal and monetary policies. For example, the government might increase its expenditures for public housing to offset slackening investment demand.

Much can be said for the positive effects of death taxes. These taxes promote greater equity among members of the same generation and probably have fewer allocation effects than other taxes. Death is impossible to avoid, and if the loopholes were closed the same might be said of death taxes. Combined with a more effective program of control over the creation of trusts and foundations, these taxes could considerably decrease the more blatant family-related industrial concentrations in our economy.

More than a generation has passed since Congress created our existing estate and gift tax structure. Although changes have been made in these laws from time to time, they have usually been specific and limited in nature. The major outlines of our estate and gift taxes—and the basic philosophy underlying them—date back to the 1900s. As L. L. Ecker Racz sees the problem, "In times of war, legislatures avoid increasing estate taxes because it would be unfair to penalize those who chance to die during the wartime emergency. In times of peace they disdain consideration of them because, as they are wont to say, these taxes pose complex issues which can be explored only when adequate time is available."[14]

In 1969, in response to the so-called taxpayer revolt, the Treasury proposed several significant improvements in the estate and gift tax laws. But most of these changes got lost in the horse trading that followed. While some changes are likely to be made during the next few years, a major restructuring of the laws is unlikely. Too much is at stake for the warriors for wealth to lie idly by. And until more Americans become knowledgeable about the economics of the rich, there will be little impetus for Congress to provide major reform of the estate tax. The reasons for this are explained further in the next chapter.

---

[14] L. L. *Ecker Racz*, The Politics and Economics of State-Local Finance (*Englewood Cliffs, N.J.: Prentice-Hall, Inc., 1970*), *p. 70.*

4
THE
WAR FOR
WEALTH–I

There are eight degrees in the giving of charity,
one higher than the other. The highest
degree . . . is to take hold of a man who has
been crushed and to give him a gift or
a loan, or to enter into partnership with him,
or to find work for him, and thus to put
him on his feet so that he will not be dependent
on his fellow men.
—MOSES BEN MAIMON

Robert Heilbroner has written that "As far back as there is history, men have dreamed of wealth: to what heights have they not reached—and to what depths have they not sunk—in quest of golden dreams! High treason and low trickery, great affairs of state and petty squabbles over an inheritance, marriage, and murder: what aspect of the tragicomedy of man has not been touched by the love of gain."[1]

Our institutions condone the war for wealth. The "clever" businessman fleeces unsuspecting consumers, the trade association lobbies to gain special favors for its members, and our political representatives follow policies designed to maximize their stay in office.

The government sector is a major source of wealth in today's society. That this is true is a tribute to our system of representation. A congressman or other official has many incentives to represent the interests of the wealthy over those of the poor. After all, a representative need only be correct *on the average*

---

[1] *Robert Heilbroner,* The Quest for Wealth *(New York: Simon & Schuster, Inc., 1956), p. 3.*

to be reelected. He is free to take a position that differs from his constituents' on a series of issues. By siding with the wealthy, he can gain their faith and their financial support. Given his income, he is likely to find that policies aiding the wealthy also benefit him. Since these policies usually favor a small group, they can be appropriately disguised behind suitable legalisms and carried out in a manner that hides their existence from the public.

In his excellent study of tax policies, Philip Stern found countless examples of specially tailored relief provisions in the tax laws. One such provision was written in such a way that it applied to only one man—Louis Mayer.

> The Louis B. Mayer provision, for example, saved Mayer $2 million; and a Washington lawyer matter-of-factly mentioned in a sidewalk conversation that his success in changing a single date in one tax measure meant a $3 million saving for his client, and that the insertion of such a technicality as a parenthetical cross-reference in another statute brought comparable savings to a second client[2]

The congressman who represents his constituents on key issues but strikes an occasional blow for the war for wealth is unlikely to be defeated in the next election.

Knowledge is costly. And most elected officials do not have the time or money to find out what their constituents think about each issue. Thus elected officials are sometimes not well informed about the wishes of their constituents. Many politicians rely on lobbyists and interest groups to articulate the views of the common man. Unfortunately, however, most such groups tend to represent the views of those with the money to finance them. This gives the wealthy a distinct advantage over the poor. Lobbyists, Washington tax attorneys, and public relations firms are expensive, and the average man finds it difficult to pay the money necessary to hire a spokesman. The war for wealth is usually fought by those with the funds to finance a campaign!

People with average incomes have few incentives to try to influence tax and expenditure policies—the returns simply

[2] *Philip M. Stern,* The Great Treasury Raid *(New York: Random House, Inc., 1964), p. 294.*

aren't great enough. Wealthy people devote resources to winning the war for wealth precisely because they expect substantial gains from policies that favor the accumulation of wealth. For example, the capital gains provision of the 1969 Tax Reform Act reduced the average tax rate paid by people under the federal income tax law by one-tenth of 1 percent for those in the $9,000–10,000 adjusted gross income bracket. For those with an adjusted gross income of $1 million or more, the rate reduction was about 23 percent.[3] Similarly, oil companies spent thousands of dollars to defend the oil import quota until its elimination in 1973, but a recent estimate suggests that this quota was worth about $5 billion to them each year.[4]

Presidential candidates are increasingly drawn to the use of flashy media techniques. To pay for them they form businessmen's councils or speak at $100-a-plate fund raising dinners. Gubernatorial candidates, congressmen, and mayors also depend on the contributions of wealthy party members to help finance their campaigns.

A LESSON IN HOME FINANCE

While contributions from wealthy benefactors are an important source of campaign funds, family fortunes also play an important role in placing candidates before the public eye. In the most detailed study ever made of campaign contributions to political candidates, the Citizens Research Foundation of Princeton, N. J., found that personal assets played an important role in the political process. For example, Governor Nelson A. Rockefeller's total spending since 1952, including the fraction of his gubernatorial campaign contributions coming from nonfamily sources, has exceeded $27 million. In 1970 alone Mr. Rockefeller spent more than $7.7 million, including at least $4.5 million from Rockefeller family members. His sister, Mrs. Abby R. Mauze, and his brothers, John D. III, David, Laurance, and Winthrop, gave him some $1.5 million. His stepmother, the late Mrs. Martha Bird, gave him $2.8 million, and

    [3] *Joseph A. Pechman,* Federal Tax Policy *(New York: W. W. Norton & Company, Inc., 1971), pp. 298–299.*
    [4] *Cabinet Task Force on Oil Import Control,* The Oil Import Question *(Washington, D.C.: U.S. Government Printing Office, 1970).*

other family members such as John D. IV contributed small amounts ($500 or less).[5]

Representative Richard L. Ottinger, heir to a plywood fortune, and James H. Scheuer, a real-estate developer, have also benefited from family finance. Mr. Ottinger received family contributions of $3.9 million in 1970. His mother, Louise, gave him almost $2.7 million; his sister, Mrs. Patricia Chernoff, gave about $844,000; and his wife, Betty Ann, contributed $225,000. Mr. Scheuer's family contributions were about $126,000.[6]

Several other candidates drew heavily on family funds. In Ohio, Howard M. Metzenbaum received $507,500 from his wife and four daughters. Norton Simon, a Los Angeles food executive, and his wife Lucille used about $1.4 million of family money, and Florida drugstore and department store owner Jack M. Eckerd invested over $1.1 million in his primary campaign for the gubernatorial nomination. As the experience of some of these candidates suggests, however, a family fortune can buy the public eye but may not buy the public vote.

Table 6 lists some of the individuals who gave more than $25,000 in campaign contributions in 1970. The list, which reflects both family contributions and payments from wealthy benefactors, is liberally sprinkled with warlords. Notice the large number of contributions from wealthy businessmen.

A new Federal Election Campaign Act, which went into effect in April 1972, limits gifts from candidates and their relatives for campaigns for representative, senator, and President to $25,000, $35,000, and $50,000, respectively. It is hoped that this will reduce the importance of "home" finance.

Although family finance has played an important role in campaigns for the Senate and House, as well as in state and local races, it pales when compared to the funds made available to candidates by conglomerates, large corporations, and other business enterprises. Over the years such support has ranged from the loan of trusted employees for political campaigns to the contribution of huge sums of money as well as corporate airplanes, recreation facilities, and products. To provide the details of this fascinating and complex story would require another book at least as long as this one.

[5] The New York Times, *April 19, 1972.*
[6] The New York Times, *April 19, 1972.*

Table 6

SELECTED LIST OF CONTRIBUTORS TO POLITICAL CAMPAIGNS WHO PAID
$25,000 OR MORE IN 1970

Contributor	Title	Company Affiliation	Family Affiliation & Recipient of Contribution	Amount of Contribution
Alva T. Bonda	Chairman	ITT Consumer Services	Former Partner with Howard Metzenbaum—Metzenbaum	$ 108,000
William M. Brinton	Lawyer	San Francisco	None—Gov. Nelson Rockefeller	$ 93,400
Patricia Chernoff	—	—	Sister—Richard Ottinger	$ 843,929
Jack M. Eckerd	Drugstore & Dept. Store Owner	Eckerd Drugs	—	$1,105,832
Leonard K. Firestone	President	Firestone Tire & Rubber Company of California	None—Richard Nixon	$ 49,250
Patrick J. Frawley, Jr.	Chairman of Exec. Committee	Schick Electric	None—Republicans	$ 39,250
Bob Hope	Comedian	—	None—Gov. Reagan	$ 25,000
Davis S. Ingalls, Jr.	Lawyer, Vice Chairman	Taft Broadcasting Co.	Cousin—mostly to Sen. Robert Taft, Jr.	$ 88,000
Francis S. Levien	President & Chairman	Universal American Corp.	None—Democrats	$ 42,000
Gustave A. Levy	Partner	Goldman, Sachs & Co.	None—Republicans	$ 41,000
Abby Rockefeller Mauze	—	—	Sister—mostly to Gov. Nelson Rockefeller	
Shirley T. Metzenbaum and daughters	—	—	Wife, daughters—Howard Metzenbaum Campaign	$ 202,000
John A. Mulcahy	President	Quigley Co.	None—Republicans	$ 507,500
				$ 147,000

Contributor	Title	Company Affiliation	Family Affiliation & Recipient of Contribution	Amount of Contribution
Max Palevsky	President	Scientific Data Systems, Inc.	None—Democrats	$ 50,000
Charles S. Payson	Director	Automation Industries, Inc.	None—Republicans	$ 32,000
Joan Whitney Payson	Vice President	New York Mets		
J. Howard Pew	Chairman	Sun Oil Co.	None—Contrib. with two sisters to Republicans	$ 54,997
Arnold M. Picker	Chairman	United Artists Corp.	None—Democrats	$ 65,000
Donald Pritzker	President	Hyatt Corp. (hotels)	None—John V. Tunney	$ 60,000
Mrs. Joseph C. Root	—	Wife of physician	None—W. C. Cramer	$ 75,000
Pierre Salinger	Vice President	Continental Air Lines	None—gave or lent to Democrats	$ 25,400
Henry Salvatori	President	Grant Oil Tool Co.	None—Republicans, Conservatives	$ 99,800
Richard Mellon Scaife	Vice President	T. Mellon & Sons	None—Republicans	$ 37,000
Samuel Schulman	President	Seattle Supersonics (Basketball Team)	None—Republicans	$ 41,250
	Chairman	San Diego Chargers (Football Team)		
Norton Simon & wife	Chairman	Hunt Foods & Industries, Inc.	None—Contrib. to his own campaign and party	$1,911,480
Frank Sinatra	Singer	—	None—Gov. Reagan and party	$ 34,500
DeWitt & Lilla Wallace	Founders & Co-Chairmen	Reader's Digest	None—Republicans, Conservatives	$ 41,700
John Hay Whitney	Head	Corinthian Broadcasting Co.	None—Republicans	$ 47,750

Source: *The New York Times*, April 19, 1972.

It becomes easier to hide the fact that political contributions are exchanged for an occasional favor as the population grows larger. Witness the enraged outcry of the media when the newspapers reported that Howard Hughes had made a "loan" to President Nixon's brother. No one knew about the "loan" at the time. When several millionaires attempted to form a group to make political contributions in 1971, they were forced to disband after public announcement resulted in widespread disapproval. Availability of funds and privacy in the dispensing of funds are important weapons in the arsenal of the warriors for wealth.

INCOME MAINTENANCE FOR THE RICH

In Chapter 1 we argued that the rich are engaged in fighting and winning a war for wealth. The tools of this war include the political power exercised through lobbyists, campaign contributions, and positions of influence at the highest levels of government; the economic power emanating from control of the nation's factories, its large corporations, and its financial community; and the social power reflected in control of the nation's educational system, its legal institutions, and its media. We also suggested that the ultimate beneficiaries of this war are the warlords, although the knights and the estate class benefit indirectly. And the guiding principle is one that will recur throughout the book—namely, the internalization of wealth. In this chapter and the following one we shall attempt to learn more about the way in which this internalization takes place.

What methods does the government use to allocate funds to the rich? First, it provides subsidies directly through programs deemed essential to the public interest. Government subsidies take several forms, including straight cash payments, tax reductions, credit aids, benefits in kind, government purchases at prices above those prevailing in the marketplace, and regulatory activities. Historically the national interest has been used to justify such diverse programs as the oil quota, interstate highway construction, urban housing, and the creation of national stockpiles of strategic materials. All of these programs have benefited the wealthy. Second, the government provides funds indirectly via programs designed for other social purposes. For example, the war on poverty has served as a vehicle for facilitating the expansion of several large companies. Third, it selects stabilization policies that benefit the rich. For example, so-called trickle-down theories designed to help the poor by stimulating business investment increase the profits of investors, usually the rich. Fourth, it opens the government payroll to a variety of people who prepare themselves for later dealings with the government. Many of these people then use their inside knowledge to procure large profits for the private companies that hire them.

The Burden of the National Interest

A look at the federal budget suggests that federal subsidies are often granted to individuals or organizations engaged in activities connected with the "national interest." An individual can get a share of these subsidies by forming a defense-related enterprise, by hiring a public relations firm to define his services as vital to the public, or by entering a firm already engaged in protecting the national interest. The importance of an institutional affiliation cannot be overemphasized. A company succeeds or fails "through no fault of its own." An individual succeeds or fails through his own efforts. Our society eschews direct subsidies to the poor as degrading, inimical to the economic system, and corrupting. Subsidies to companies headed by the wealthy are defended as necessary to preserve economically viable enterprises, to reduce "hardships to displaced employees," or "to maintain competition" in heavily concentrated industries.

As Domhoff points out, "Contrary to the stereotypes, most members of the American upper class are and always have been hard-working people, even at the richest levels. The American upper class is a business aristocracy and business is its primary concern."[7] As a result, subsidy programs to help the wealthy for such purposes as transportation, manpower, price support, international trade, housing, and education are largely business based.

[7] G. William Domhoff, Who Rules America (Englewood Cliffs, N.J.: Prentice-Hall, Inc., 1967), p. 31.

In a 1971 speech President Nixon argued that

> The goal of the American system is not to guarantee every-
> body a living, it is to guarantee everybody an opportunity
> —a fair chance to be rewarded for his work. The American
> people will not be denied that goal by those who could
> work or those who could take training but prefer to take it
> easy. . . . No job is a menial job if it opens the door to a
> lifetime of work and the development of self-reliance. . . .
> The most menial job I can think of is the one held by the
> able bodied person who makes a career out of living off
> the hard earned dollars of his neighbor.

Shortly thereafter several states showed support for the President's policies by reducing their welfare rolls. The total
dropped from state rolls reached a new high of 84,000 in July
alone. New Jersey dropped 10,800, California 8,600, Oregon
6,500, New York 4,900, and Kansas 4,200.[8]

At about the same time, the $115,000-a-year president of
Lockheed Aircraft, Daniel Houghton, appeared before the
Senate Committee on Banking, Housing, and Urban Affairs.
His purpose was to ask for a federal loan guarantee. His
defense was the national interest. Employment at Lockheed
had fallen from a post-World War II peak of 99,250 in the
summer of 1969 to 71,700 in May 1971. Bankruptcy of the
company might have forced a further reduction of 10,000. It
also threatened the financial stability of several large banks.[9]

Lockheed's problems resulted from both adverse circumstances and bad judgment. The company submitted a below-
cost bid for the C-5A military transport. After receiving the
contract it experienced cost overruns of almost $2 billion. Rising
expenses, due largely to unexpected production costs, also
affected several of Lockheed's other military programs. The
company asked the Pentagon to absorb the higher costs, but
the Pentagon balked and instead forced Lockheed to absorb
over $200 million in excess costs.[10] With about 80 percent of

[8] The New York Times, *November 13, 1971.*
[9] *U.S. Senate, Committee on Banking, Housing, and Urban Affairs,
Emergency Loan Guarantee Legislation (Washington, D.C.: U.S. Government Printing Office, July 1971), p. 213.*
[10] Loan Guarantee Legislation, *p. 214.*

its sales going to the government and about 90 percent of its government sales going to the Defense Department, Lockheed responded to its true owner's demands—although its stockholders expressed dissatisfaction.

At about the same time Lockheed fell into difficulty with its Tristar jet. The company had not produced for the civilian aircraft market since it lost $121 million on the Electra aircraft. Executives of several other companies warned that the introduction of the Tristar was premature, and Lockheed's management knew that McDonnell Douglas would have a DC-10 airbus ready long before Lockheed could complete the Tristar. Nonetheless, President Houghton went ahead with production.

The day of reckoning came in February 1971 with the bankruptcy of Rolls Royce, which was collaborating with Lockheed in the production of the jet. As Houghton put it, "Delays in the Rolls-Royce program decisively increased the company's cash requirements and it became apparent that a restructuring of the financing plan would be necessary."[11] The banks had already committed loan funds to Lockheed to the tune of $400 million, and further loans would be forthcoming only if they were guaranteed by the government. So Houghton, formerly a supporter of free enterprise, went to Congress to advocate a new subsidy program for business.

At issue was the integrity of the private-enterprise system. To many economists a company's success or failure in the marketplace reflects its skill in allocating scarce resources. Firms that operate efficiently earn profits, while those that do not go out of business. In 1960 about 15,000 smaller companies and about 169,000 consumers faced bankruptcy. But Lockheed refused to be treated as just another statistic. Its civil-service status entitled it to more!

Such a request for government aid by a major company is largely unprecedented in American business history. It serves as an excellent example of how the national interest can be used to justify protection of the incomes of a select few. While it is true that the jobs of 10,000 employees were presumably on the line, it should be noted that no one blinked when Lockheed laid off 17,500 employees between the summer of 1969 and

[11] Loan Guarantee Legislation, *p. 220.*

May 1971. But more was at stake here. A Lockheed failure meant a possible bankruptcy for several banks and a number of Lockheed subcontractors, and loans to several other aircraft companies might be called.

President Nixon and other officials in Washington thought these events might trigger a financial crisis. Yet many economists believed that the business retrenchment that might have been caused by a Lockheed failure was likely to be small and that the negative effects could have been tempered through appropriate monetary and fiscal policies. Moreover, a myriad of socially useful projects ranging from pollution reduction to traffic control awaited the skills of the soon-to-be-released employees.

That Houghton stayed, that Congress granted the loan, that Lockheed was permitted to build the C-5A transport after experiencing average unit cost increases from $27 million to $60 million per plane, that there were reportedly 127 unresolved deficiencies per aircraft—these are poignant examples of the burden of the national interest.

Rich Man, Poor Man

Since the 1930s income redistribution to the poor has been recognized as an acceptable activity for government. The first major federal income maintenance programs were created by the 1935 Social Security Act. This act contained programs of a social insurance nature, such as social security, and welfare programs, such as public assistance. In 1971 more than 27.3 million people received benefits of over $76.2 billion from the Old Age, Survivors, and Disability Trust Funds.[12] And 24.2 million recipients of public welfare received over $10.8 billion in federal public-assistance payments.[13] Transfer programs of this type that make payments *directly* to the beneficiary have never been liked by the warriors for wealth. They offer little opportunity for internalization of wealth.

Since men first accepted the idea of a leader, the public budget has been a source of wealth to a select few. Adam Smith put the issue well:

[12] Social Security Bulletin, 35, 7 (*Washington, D.C.: U.S. Government Printing Office, July 1972*), 37, 39.
[13] Social Security Bulletin (*July 1972*), p. 53.

It is the highest impertinence and presumption, therefore, in kings and ministers, to pretend to watch over the economy of private people, and to restrain their expense, either by sumptuary laws, or by prohibiting the importation of foreign luxuries. They are themselves always, and without any exception, the greatest spendthrifts in the society. . . . If their own extravagance does not ruin the state, that of their subjects never will.[14]

Although the budget of the United States does not contain an allocation for kings, our key officials have not done badly. The fiscal-year budget for 1973 lists Presidential compensation of $250,000; the White House Office is to receive almost $9.8 million, and the executive mansion another $1.3 million. This does not include $700,000 for special assistants and $1.5 million for special projects. Nor does it take account of payments to other agencies located in the Executive Office of the President.[15] To this must be added $505 million in payments for the operation of Congress and $189 million for the expenditures of the judicial branch.

Nonetheless, the direct incomes paid to our politicians for "services rendered" must be counted as small potatoes compared to the sums paid out under several programs designed to redistribute income to the wealthy. Farm programs, housing and airlines subsidies, research and development contracts, and a host of other programs transfer billions of dollars to a fortunate few.

The wealthy manage to benefit from redistribution programs even when they are designed to help the poor. Consider the "war on poverty." Countless consulting firms and other research outfits have sought financial assistance from the poverty agency. In 1970 alone the Office of Economic Opportunity spent over $71 million for research and development grants, and over $28 million for training and technical-assistance payments. These figures exclude contracts and grants issued by the Head Start and Job Corps Programs.[16]

[14] *Adam Smith,* The Wealth of Nations *(New York: Modern Library, Inc., 1937),* p. 831.
[15] The Budget of the United States Government, Fiscal Year 1973 *(Washington, D.C.: U.S. Government Printing Office, 1973),* p. 205.
[16] *Subcommittee on Appropriations, House of Representatives,* Department of Health, Education, and Welfare, Appropriations for 1970, *Part 8 (Washington, D.C.: U.S. Government Printing Office, 1969),* p. 71.

To appreciate the extent of industry participation in the "war on poverty," however, we must look beyond the narrow confines of research and development. Table 7 shows the broad range of management activities performed by private industry and the cost of these services from November 1966 to April 1967.

These amounts are not very large compared to the $1.6 billion allocated to the poverty agency for the 1966–1967 fiscal year. They become important when we recognize how much money a few companies earned by assisting in the "war on poverty." The figures suggest that fighting poverty is good business.

Job Corps training centers provide vocational education

Table 7

SUMMARY OF PRIVATE INDUSTRY PARTICIPATION IN OFFICE
OF ECONOMIC OPPORTUNITY ACTIVITIES, OFFICE OF
MANAGEMENT FUNCTIONS
(Excludes Contracts and Grants)

Function	Number of Private Organizations	Dollar Value of Contracts Granted, November 1966 to April 1967
Job Corps Urban Center Operations	21	$147,000,000
Management consulting	7	197,000
Research and evaluations	23	1,750,000
Professional accounting, auditing, legal services	246	2,500,000
OEO housekeeping activities	409	465,000
Data processing	8	546,000
Training	12	1,100,000
Miscellaneous	18	539,000
Total	744	$154,097,000

Source: Subcommittee on Employment, Manpower, and Poverty, Senate Committee on Labor and Public Welfare, *Examination of the War on Poverty, Staff and Consultants Report* (Washington, D.C.: U.S. Government Printing Office, August 1967).

and training for low-income unemployed high school dropouts between the ages of 16 and 21. Of the $1.6 billion budgeted for the Office of Economic Opportunity in fiscal year 1966–1967, $212 million was allocated for Job Corps centers. The $147 million shown in the table represents over 70 percent of the Job Corps budget, and this was paid out primarily to private profit-making companies for management of the centers.

Job Corps men's centers are large-scale operations. According to one consultant for the poverty agency, "No company which is not at least in the over $100 million annual gross receipts class has yet received a men's center contract. Significantly, though, small and medium-sized companies comprise more than half the companies which sought such contracts." As the consultant defines these terms, a small company is one with fewer than 500 employees and a medium sized company is one with a well-known name and gross income of around $5 million.[17] Considering the objectives of the war on poverty, it is surprising to find so much money going to the handful of well-known companies shown in Table 8.

The consultant's rationale for this situation rests on the advantages these companies enjoy. Government contracts not only are costly but also take time and effort to obtain. Proposals submitted to the Job Corps cost anywhere from $15,000 to $150,000 to prepare. Experience is necessary to write a professional grant, to set up administrative procedures acceptable to government officials, and to establish adequate methods for safeguarding funds. The consultant also found that smaller companies lack the experience and the aggressiveness necessary for contract negotiation. As a result, many are inflexible in responding to governmental requirements. This explanation is not unique to the Job Corps programs, though; it is applicable to a broad range of governmental programs, including housing, road building, foreign aid, and defense.

A relatively unknown source of subsidy to the rich is the federal reclamation program, which provides for the construction of dams and canals to irrigate otherwise worthless acreage.

[17] *Subcommittee on Employment, Manpower, and Poverty, U.S. Senate, Examination of the War on Poverty, August 1967, p. 149.*

Table 8

DOLLAR VALUE OF JOB CORPS CONTRACTS

Period Contract is in Force	Name of Company	Size of Contract	Purpose
7/ 1/68– 6/30/70	Economics Systems Corp. (Avco Corp.)	$ 7,782,480	Poland Springs Center for Women
7/ 1/68– 6/30/69	Litton Systems, Inc.	10,121,200	Parks Job Corps Center & Misc.
8/11/67–10/10/70	Graflex, Inc.	32,102,949	Breckinridge Center for Men
10/ 1/68–12/31/69	Thiokol Chemical	7,675,218	Clearfield Urban Center & Misc.
9/16/67–12/ 1/70	Westinghouse Learning Corp.	23,151,995	Atterbury Job Corps Center & Misc.
2/17/69– 6/30/70	Volt Information Systems	5,806,742	Misc. Technical Functions
7/ 1/67– 6/30/69	Northern Michigan University	3,642,723	Marquette Women's Jobs Corps Center
11/22/67– 6/30/69	Philco-Ford Corp.	4,850,896	Gutherie Women's Job Corps Center
7/ 1/68– 6/30/70	YWCA of New York	4,131,500	Job Corps Women's Residential Training Corps
7/ 1/67– 6/30/70	YWCA of Los Angeles	5,570,603	Women's Training Center
1/ 1/68–12/31/69	YWCA of Jersey City	7,395,000	Jersey City Job Corps
3/10/68– 3/10/70	Alpha Kappa Alpha Sorority	3,910,500	Cleveland Center for Women
7/ 1/67– 6/30/70	General Learning Corp.	9,722,325	Clinton Center
7/ 1/67– 6/30/69	Delta Education Corp.	6,745,000	St. Louis Job Corps Center
5/ 1/69– 6/30/70	Texas Educational Foundation	19,384,700	McKinney & Gary Job Corps Centers
10/ 1/67– 9/30/68	RCA Service Co.	12,093,579	McCoy & Keystone Job Corps Centers
11/ 1/68– 8/31/70	National Education Association	1,393,446	Expose Teachers to Job Corps Program
7/ 1/67– 6/30/69	Educational Associates, Inc.	2,558,176	Services in Connection with Project Upward Bound
7/ 1/67– 6/30/69	Burroughs Corp.	9,579,400	Omaha Women's Job Corps Center
11/29/67– 6/30/70	Training Corp. of America	5,515,100	Excelsior Springs Job Corps Center for Women
8/ 8/67–12/31/68	U. S. Industries	10,429,000	Custer Job Corps Center for Men
9/ 7/67– 9/30/69	Xerox Corp.	3,502,956	Huntington Women's Job Corps Center
2/16/68– 8/ 1/69	Volt Technical Corp.	2,447,647	Misc. Management Functions
5/20/68–12/31/68	Leo Kramer Associates	1,399,615	Misc. Management Functions
4/ 1/68– 6/30/70	Packard Bell Electronics	8,594,173	Albuquerque and Charleston Job Corps Centers for Women
4/ 3/68– 4/30/70	Policy Management Systems	1,486,981	N.E. Regional Training Center for Vista
6/29/68– 8/31/69	Educational Projects, Inc.	3,834,592	Head Start Supplementary

Source: House of Representatives, Departments of Labor and Health, Education, and Welfare, *Appropriations for 1970*, Part 8 (Washington, D.C.: U.S. Government Printing Office, 1969), pp. 73–92.

The program results in substantial appreciation in the value of the land to be irrigated and provides an ongoing flow of water to the residents of the area. Such programs tend to benefit the wealthy. Consider the case of California's Imperial Valley. To irrigate an otherwise arid dust bowl, water is brought in through a $30 million canal from the $175 million Hoover Dam. One author estimates that the water increases the value of an acre of land by about $700, and he finds that more than half the irrigated acreage is owned by holders of more than 160 acres—two-thirds by absentees. Among the large holders of land are such giants as Purex Corp., United Fruit, and Irvine Land Co.[18]

A Matter of License

Many functions of government result in an implicit subsidy to the rich. Few people recognize, for example, that the licensing power of federal agencies permits the government to make or break millionaires. Licensing restricts the number of firms that may perform a given service. When the Federal Communications Commission grants a radio license to a station, this represents a grant of monopoly power over a particular radio frequency. The license has a monetary value that is often worth several million dollars. Similarly, the government issues licenses for imports and exports, to aircraft pilots, and for a host of other activities. No accounts are kept of the value of these licenses and no periodic review is conducted to determine whether they are made to the rich or to the poor. Doctors, lawyers, nurses, teachers, chiropodists, and others derive benefits from the "licenses" they are granted. Yet no one accuses them of receiving a subsidy from the government. And no one considers the companies that receive patent rights from the federal government as recipients of a federal dole. Nonetheless, the government's power to limit entry constitutes an important tool in the war for wealth.

[18] *Peter Barnes, "Water Water for the Wealthy," The New Republic, 164, 18, 2941 (May 8, 1971), 9.*

5
THE
WAR FOR
WEALTH–II

The free man will ask neither what his country
can do for him nor what he can do for
his country. He will ask rather "What can
I and my compatriots do through government"
to help us discharge our individual respon-
sibilities, to achieve our several goals
and purposes, and above all to protect
our freedom?
—MILTON FRIEDMAN

While some politicians and
newspaper columnists go to great lengths to remind us that
public-welfare payments take a healthy bite out of the federal
tax dollar, surprisingly little is said about farm subsidy programs. Yet such programs are costly. In the period from 1956
to 1970, for example, federal outlays for farm price support
programs and related payments averaged $3.1 billion per year.
And from 1968 to 1970 they rose to over $5 billion.[1]

The public budget does not tell the full story, however, since
the farm subsidy is designed to raise the price of farm products
above that paid in an unregulated market. Charles Schultze, a
well-known economist, suggests that actual prices might have
been 15 percent lower if the support programs had not been in
effect. Schultze estimates that in 1969, for example, the same
volume of farm produce could have been obtained by consumers for about $7 billion less. After allowing for the amounts
consumed by farmers and for exports, the prices paid by con-

---

[1] *Charles L. Schultze, "The Distribution of Farm Subsidies," in Ken-*
neth Boulding and Martin Pfaff (eds.), Redistribution to the Rich and the
Poor *(Belmont, Calif.: Wadsworth Publishing, 1972), p. 94.*

sumers if no program had been in effect might have been $4.5 billion lower. Adding together the direct budgetary costs of $5 billion and the indirect costs (in the form of higher prices) of $4.5 billion, we get a total subsidy to farmers of $9.5 billion. By comparison, the much faulted welfare program cost the taxpayer slightly over $10 billion in 1969.[2]

Why aren't farm subsidy payments a source of dissatisfaction among taxpayers? Following the argument in Chapter 4 that subsidies must be business-related to be acceptable, we might suppose that some taxpayers support farm payments as a reward for effort. After all, small farmers used to constitute the backbone of the nation and it might be worth something to keep them in business. Moreover, since median family income of the nonfarm population is higher than that of farm families—$9,600 compared to $6,400 in 1969—a farm subsidy program might be defended on the grounds that it provides a welfare payment to those willing to work but barely able to eke out a living.

It might be, but it isn't. Farm subsidies are not distributed in relation to a farmer's *income* but rather in terms of what his farm *produces*. The greater its output, the larger the subsidy. Since approximately 568,000 farms (about one-fifth of the total) sell roughly three-fourths of all farm products, the bulk of the subsidies go to farmers in the top income fifth—those with incomes of over $20,000 in 1969. And the 1.5 million farmers with incomes averaging about $8,000 account for only 5 percent of farm sales and a similar share of farm subsidy payments.

Perhaps the main reason why farm payments have not been subject to the same criticism as welfare programs is that many critics have simply despaired of being able to eliminate them and have turned their attention elsewhere. The farm lobby is one of the oldest and best organized in Congress. And farm subsidy beneficiaries have been highly vocal and well financed. Moreover, the farm programs are complex and hard for the public to understand. In fact, it isn't easy to talk to the taxpayer about what prices "might" have been or to invoke an

---

[2] *Schultze, p. 95.*

image of a welfare recipient mounted high on the seat of an International Harvester tractor. Few people realize that J. G. Boswell Co. of California received $4.4 million in subsidies in 1970 or that Tenneco and U.S. Sugar Corp. received $1.1 million each.[3]

The farm support program provides a fine example of the advantages of privatizing wealth. Most wealthy recipients of these funds do not talk about the amounts they receive in public. The taxpayer's willingness to pay for price supports is assumed, no further discussion is really necessary, and woe to the Presidential or congressional candidate who thinks otherwisc!

AGAINST THE GRAIN

Most farm subsidy programs provide a large portion of their benefits to members of the estate class and to the knights, although a few of the very wealthy participate in the handouts. Some programs are tailor-made to the needs of several large companies and their stockholders. These rarely reach the front page of the local newspaper. One exception, however, is the now defunct export subsidy that briefly caught the public eye after the recent sale of wheat to the Soviet Union. The export subsidy provides a good example of how governmental policies can enable a few warriors for wealth to internalize the benefits of a governmental action at a substantial cost to the public. Its demise reflects the importance of keeping information on federal subsidies out of the hands of the public.

The story begins in early 1972, when as a result of a gigantic crop failure the Soviet Union was forced to buy large amounts of wheat from U.S. farmers. Because the magnitude of the sale was not made public, many southwestern farmers sold their crops at prices that later turned out to be as much as 65 percent below the world market price. A farmer in Haven, Texas, for example, might have received $1.30 per bushel

[3] Peter Barnes, "*The Vanishing Small Farmer*," The New Republic, *164, 24, 2946 (June 12, 1971),* 23.

before the Department of Agriculture made public the size of the deal with the Soviets, only to watch the price of a bushel rise to $2.06 shortly afterward.

Six big exporters that secretly negotiated with the Soviet Union at the end of June had no such problem. While the July 18 issue of the *Southwestern Miller*, a journal popular among farmers, was telling its readership that the Russians planned to purchase about 100 million bushels of wheat, these six grain exporters had already sold 267 million bushels to the Soviet Union.[4] These companies exported about 90 percent of the total grain leaving this country.

To appreciate the role of the public as a silent partner in the U.S.-Soviet wheat deal, let us briefly review the history of the wheat export subsidy. This was adopted after World War II in a period of large surpluses in order to assist U.S. farmers in trading on the world market. Wheat exporters would sell at the going world market price (usually less than the U.S. market price), and the federal government would make up the difference and allow a reasonable profit to the exporters. Such subsidies have been provided since the early 1950s.

Here is how the export subsidy would have worked on July 13, 1972, as reported by Walter Cronkite of CBS News:

> The domestic price of hard red winter wheat was $1.77 per bushel. The U.S. export price . . . was $1.64 per bushel, a difference of 13 cents a bushel. So the government would have paid the grain sellers 13 cents in subsidy for each bushel of wheat registered for sale to the Russians, on that day. Now the key word there is "registered," because under the government system the amount of the subsidy was determined on the day the grain exporters registered, or officially notified the Agriculture Department of the sale. . . . The government by failing to terminate or otherwise adjust the subsidy when the domestic price skyrocketed, opened the way to windfall profits . . . the price of wheat was shooting up, pushed by the Russian deal, and the government maintained the subsidies. So it was possible for an exporter whose cost was $1.77 to hold off registering the sale with the govern-

[4] *CBS News, September 27, 1972.*

ment while the subsidy went up. He could then, for example,
notify the government of the sale on August 14th, when
the subsidy was 36 cents per bushel, instead of 13 cents—
an excess profit of 23 cents per bushel. In fact, on August 14th,
according to the Agriculture Department, the big grain
traders registered 58 million bushels . . .[5]

With public criticism mounting, the Department of Agriculture ended the subsidy system, although not without providing a final tribute to the warriors for wealth. For five more business days the big exporters could continue to receive a subsidy—then equal to 47 cents—for hard red winter wheat. The sum paid out during this period amounted to over $77 million for over 166 million registered bushels of wheat. Critics of the subsidy charge that the excess profits from the wheat export deal ranged into tens of millions of dollars. Although one of the six companies—Cargill Inc.—later announced that it did not benefit from the wheat sale, the remaining five companies have remained silent about their profits, preferring to keep their public affairs as private as possible.

The United States–Soviet Union wheat deal provides a textbook illustration of how the benefits of a large public program can be internalized. The export subsidy is complex and largely ignored by the public. The costs of the subsidy are diffuse and difficult to identify. The program was an old and established one. And strong connections existed between the people who administer agricultural programs in the federal government and those who benefit from them.

THE DIVIDENDS OF GROWTH

For years, many warriors for wealth have argued that the whole population benefits from policies designed to raise aggregate demand. During the 1950s, President Dwight D. Eisenhower's advisers advocated a trickle-down approach to poverty. Advocates of this theory believe that business investment leads to long-range benefits for the entire population.

[5] *CBS News, September 27, 1972.*

Years of slow growth and grave disparities of income failed to reverse this view. In 1958, John Galbraith wrote, "Few things are more evident in modern social history than the decline of interest in inequality as an economic issue."[6]

The sixties gave rise to "the new economics" and with it hopes for a more egalitarian society. This was to be accomplished via policies designed to stimulate growth and redistribute income. Unfortunately, however, the new economists soon came to the old realization that under the present political system the income distribution is difficult to change. Says Arthur Okun, a "new" economist, "As I read the 1969 record, it provides a sober reminder that, until we win a long uphill battle of public education: a) the Congress will not improve the tax system without seriously impairing its revenue-raising capabilities and b) the strategy of packaging tax reform and tax stabilization as a tie-in sale can be very costly."[7]

With the new economists constrained in their attempts to improve the income distribution, many put their faith in economic growth as the new source of social justice. Increases in the total pie would give everybody more to eat. Advocates of this approach—members of the maximization-of-growth school —distinguish it from the trickle-down theory. They stress the need to increase aggregate demand, rather than merely augmenting business investment. They also urge that the expanded tax revenues resulting from economic growth be devoted to improved social programs. By 1963 President John F. Kennedy had accepted the growth-maximization approach and was pressing hard for a tax cut designed to raise aggregate demand. The tax bill he eventually received was not egalitarian, however; instead, it contained several provisions beneficial to the wealthy.

The growth-maximization approach is clearly stated in the 1964 Council of Economic Advisors report: ". . . the advance of standards of living depends on the rate of growth of productivity per capita, and this, in turn, depends on science

---

[6] *John Kenneth Galbraith,* The Affluent Society *(Boston: Houghton Mifflin Company, 1958), p. 72.*

[7] *Arthur Okun, "Communications: Two Views of the New Economics,"* The New Republic, *162, 7, 2877 (February 14, 1970), 20.*

and technology, capital accumulation, and investments in human resources. . . . Growth also expands the resources available to governments and private organizations to finance specific programs against poverty."[8]

Policies designed to increase economic growth frequently provide windfalls for the wealthy. One growth-promoting device that is particularly attractive to warriors for wealth is accelerated depreciation. This tax provision permits a company to deduct the depreciation of a piece of equipment from its corporate income tax at a greater-than-normal rate. Under the federal income tax laws depreciation is an offset against the revenues of a firm; a high depreciation deduction thus enables a firm to show a higher posttax profit than would otherwise have been possible in the first few years after it purchases a new piece of equipment.

A second growth-stimulating provision of the tax law that is beneficial to business is the investment tax credit. Under the 1962 law, for example, anyone who purchased certain types of capital goods, primarily machinery with a long service life, could subtract from his income tax an amount equal to 7 percent of what he paid. A taxpayer who purchased a $100,000 machine with a service life of eight years could subtract $7,000 from his income tax in the year of purchase. Investments in tangible personal property for certain types of buildings were considered eligible for the tax credit. This credit was eliminated by Congress in 1969 but has since been reenacted.

Figure 8 shows how profits fared during the "soaring sixties," reflecting the effects of accelerated depreciation, the investment tax credit, and other economic forces. Corporate profits rose by 83 percent from 1961 to 1968. By comparison, the average salary of an accountant rose by about 31 percent during the same period, the average salary of clerical workers rose by about 28 percent, and engineering technicians' salaries rose only 23 percent. Nonwhite teenage unemployment fell from 27.5 percent in 1961 to 25 percent in 1969. And many

[8] Economic Report of the President, 1964 *(Washington, D.C.: U.S. Government Printing Office), p. 74.*

Figure 8
CORPORATE PROFITS, 1961–1968[1]

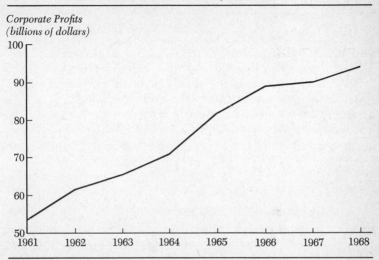

Corporate Profits
(billions of dollars)

Source: *Economic Report of the President,* 1970 (Washington, D.C.: U.S. Government Printing Office), Table C-73.

[1]Includes capital consumption allowances (estimates of depreciation, obsolescence, and destruction or loss of physical assets).

blacks found their incomes remaining substantially below those of their white counterparts. The soaring sixties brought social planners back to the crashing reality that many low-income families do not participate in the gains of our economic system.

In a post-mortem recently published by the Brookings Institution, an eminent group of economists analyzed the sixties this way:

It is now clear—as it was not in the early 1960's— that even full employment does not solve the job problems of the poor. Pushing unemployment down to 3.5 percent in the late 1960's induced inflationary shortages in some manpower categories well before it eliminated unemployment among the least skilled. Furthermore, the spread between the un-

employment rate of the most employable (prime age men)
and that of the least employable (women and teenagers, especially if they are black) has been increasing.
Manpower training programs in the 1960's also proved to be
considerably less successful than had been hoped . . .
when unemployment was high, subsidized training programs
in private industry tended to shrink, since employers were
laying off workers generally . . . when unemployment was
low, trainees were mainly the hard-core unemployed. Programs that succeeded in retraining and placing a high
percentage of trainees . . . were those whose trainees were
chiefly prime age men with some recent work experience.
Success rates were far lower for women, teenagers, and men
who had little education and had not worked for a
long time.[9]

Of course, it can be argued that during the same period the
number of poor decreased, more money was put into social
programs, and the unemployment rate fell. But these points
do not negate the fact that increases in aggregate demand,
especially those that make their initial impact on business, are
highly beneficial to the wealthy.

In 1971 President Nixon suggested a "game plan" designed
to get the economy moving. The trickle-down theory was
implicit in his approach. By lifting the surcharge on automobiles and encouraging additional business investment, the
President hoped to improve the unemployment rate sufficiently
to increase his chance of reelection. The President was warned
that the automobile industry would simply sop up excess
demand through overtime. He also knew that some firms were
already operating with excess capacity. Despite these facts
Nixon insisted on a program with obvious benefits to one
industry. The game plan was put into effect during the spring
and summer of 1971. As many economists had predicted, it
barely affected the unemployment rate. Nonetheless, corporate profits went up almost immediately.

The persistent reappearance of the trickle-down theory as

[9] *Charles L. Schultze et al.*, Setting National Priorities: The 1972
Budget *(Washington, D.C.: The Brookings Institution, 1971), p. 198.*

a guide for national policy seems to support our earlier contention that the war for wealth is an ongoing one. Trickle-down theories and their sophisticated variants are likely to be with us for years to come.

TOWARD A JOB CORPS FOR THE WEALTHY

Federal service provides many opportunities for people who wish to receive training in how to get rich through government. Although not explicitly stated as such, government "training programs" serve as an entry point to the road to wealth. An ambitious young person enters the federal government either in a civil-service job or as a political appointee. While in the federal service, he or she gains experience in how the government operates. He learns which people make decisions involving private industry and, in some cases, actually makes the decisions himself. If he plays his cards right, he serves the interests of the warriors for wealth.

This strategy increases a person's value to private industry. By learning how the government operates and then leaving it, he can raise his income. Similarly, by doing an industry a favor while employed by the government, an individual can enhance his future earning potential.

An interchange between business and government personnel occurs at almost all levels and branches of government. In the various agencies, bureaus, and departments, in the CIA and the military, in Congress and the judiciary branch, and at the highest levels of the executive branch, the government actively solicits businessmen to enter the federal ranks. The formal rationale seems to be that by virtue of their success in industry these businessmen can introduce new and, it is hoped, innovative techniques into government operations.

Perhaps the most comprehensive study of the business-government exchange was conducted by G. William Domhoff, who found that the upper class and the power elite play an important role in the operation of government. Examining the composition of the President's cabinet, Domhoff identified the positions of secretary of state, defense, commerce, and the Treasury as heavily dominated by people from the upper class

and the power elite. It is useful to see whether Domhoff's conclusions, which apply to the period from 1932 to 1964, are
still relevant.

Consider the eight secretaries of state who served during
the period under consideration. Domhoff found that five of
these eight—Edward Stettinius, George C. Marshall, Dean
Acheson, John Foster Dulles, and Christian Herter—were
listed in the Social Register. Three were corporation lawyers,
and one of these was a partner with J. P. Morgan. Since 1964
one more secretary of state has served, William P. Rogers, and
he certainly must be labeled a member of the power elite.
Almost all of these gentlemen have gone back into private
practice, some representing their clients before the federal
agencies for which they previously worked.

Domhoff also found that of the 13 men who have served as
secretary of defense or secretary of war since 1932, eight have
been listed in the Social Register. The remainder were bankers
and corporation executives. Since his study, Clark Clifford,
Melvin R. Laird, and Elliot L. Richardson have served as
secretary of defense. Clifford is a successful lawyer and director of a bank and oil company, while Laird was a congressman
from Wisconsin. Richardson, previously secretary of health,
education, and welfare (HEW) and later to become attorney
general, is a member of an old, established family and is frequently referred to as a "Boston Brahmin." Of the seven secretaries of the Treasury between 1932 and 1964, William H.
Woodin, Dean Acheson, Henry Morgenthau, Jr., and C.
Douglas Dillon were all members of the upper class, while
two others, John W. Snyder and Robert B. Anderson, were
members of the power elite. The addition of David M. Kennedy, a Chicago banker, John B. Connally, a wealthy Texan
politician, and George P. Shultz, a college professor, to the list
adds three more members of the power elite.

Of 11 attorneys general, Domhoff found four who could be
accorded upper-class status—Francis B. Biddle, Herbert
Brownell, Robert F. Kennedy, and Nicholas deB. Katzenbach.
William P. Rogers is a member of the power elite, and the
remaining six are lawyers with experience in city and state
politics. Nixon's appointments of John N. Mitchell, a Wall

Street lawyer specializing in mutual funds, and Elliot L. Richardson, mentioned earlier, added two more warriors for wealth to the list.

The addition of Maurice H. Stans, Peter G. Peterson (ex-chairman of Bell & Howell), and Frederick B. Dent to the list of secretaries of commerce increases the total of power elite secretaries from four to seven. And the addition of Elliot L. Richardson and Caspar W. Weinberger to the list of secretaries of HEW raises the number of scions of wealth heading that department from three out of six to four out of eight. (Since HEW is a new agency, the list begins in 1953 rather than 1932. Nonetheless, a substantial number of warriors for wealth have served as its secretary during the past several years.)

President Nixon's fondness for businessmen has led to the appointments of Claude S. Brinegar as secretary of transportation Roy Ash (president of Litton Industries) to head the Office of Management and Budget, and Earl L. Butz (ex-dean at Purdue University and director of two agribusinesses) as secretary of agriculture. Nixon's other appointments have included James T. Lynn, an attorney skilled in corporate acquisitions (Housing and Urban Development); Walter Hickel, a millionaire and ex-governor of Alaska (Interior); and Rogers C. B. Morton, ex-chairman of the Republican National Committee (Interior).

By almost any standards the Nixon appointees must be counted as members of the power elite. And the number of appointees with Harvard degrees might surprise even G. William Domhoff. In one day alone Nixon announced the appointment of three Harvard graduates—Ash, Weinberger, and Richardson. Shortly thereafter he added Lynn to the list.

Federal training programs for the wealthy may be found in thousands of locations scattered throughout the federal departments. For example, Clarence Palmby, assistant secretary of agriculture for international affairs, left the Department of Agriculture on June 7, 1972, to join Continental Grain Company. Carroll Brunthaver, an ex-employee of another grain exporter (the Cooke Company), replaced Palmby. On June 30, Clifford Pulvermacher resigned as general manager of the

Department of Agriculture's Export Marketing Service to
become the Washington representative for another large grain
exporter, Bunge Corp. And in true musical-chairs fashion,
George Shanklin, who had been Washington representative for
Bunge, joined the Export Marketing Service.[10] It would take
a small computer to account for all of the changes over the
past 20 years!

The importance of federal service as a steppingstone to
wealth and power is illustrated by the case of Clarence Palmby,
who participated in the U.S.-Soviet wheat deal of 1972. Palmby
received a job offer from Continental Grain in early March of
that year. On April 5 he signed a contract for purchase of a
luxury cooperative apartment in New York City, listing four top
officials of Continental Grain as references. Three days later
he was in Moscow, playing a key role in negotiating the grain
sale. On May 9 he met with an important Soviet trade official
in Washington, and on June 8, less than a month later, Palmby
went to work for Continental Grain. Shortly thereafter Continental concluded a 150-million-bushel wheat sale with the
Soviet Union, almost two months before news of the sale
reached farmers in the Southwest. Palmby's experiences provide a vivid illustration of how the federal government can
serve as a prime training ground for people wishing to improve
their contacts—and their incomes.

Opportunities also abound in the regulatory agencies. These
agencies, together with the various departments of the executive branch, furnish most of the training positions for potential
warriors for wealth. There are over 30 regulatory agencies,
and their power extends to virtually every aspect of the
economy. Among the best known are the Atomic Energy Commission (AEC), the Federal Aviation Agency (FAA), the
Federal Communications Commission (FCC), the Federal
Power Commission (FPC), the Federal Trade Commission
(FTC), the Interstate Commerce Commission (ICC), and
the Securities and Exchange Commission (SEC).

The young lawyer just starting out may wish to begin his
career at the prestigious SEC or at the National Labor Rela-

---

[10] *CBS News, September 27, 1972.*

tions Board (NLRB). A short stint at either place makes him
a valuable commodity to a law firm. At higher levels those who
have served with a regulatory agency can usually move from
the agency into the regulated industry with a substantial
accompanying pay boost. Similarly, at the very top of a
regulatory agency the commissioners receive substantial sums
to perform "services" for the businesses they regulate—including payments for attendance at speeches, panel discussions,
and conferences.

It would be impossible to list all of the opportunities provided by regulatory agencies. But one example is in order. In
a recent study of the ICC, Robert Fellmeth checked on the
whereabouts of the last 11 commissioners. He found that eight
were directly or indirectly involved in operations connected
with the ICC. The remaining three are now retired. Fellmeth's
findings appear in Table 9.

Clearly the ICC operates as a training ground for high
officials in the transportation industry. According to Fellmeth,

Table 9

WHEREABOUTS OF ICC EX-COMMISSIONERS

Name	Year Left ICC	Current Position
Owen Clarke	1958	Chesapeake and Ohio–Baltimore and Ohio Railroad, vice-president
Robert W. Minor	1958	Penn Central, senior vice president
Anthony Arpaia	1960	REA Express, vice president (retired)
John H. Winchell	1960	retired
Donald McPherson	1962	ICC practitioner
Clyde E. Herring	1964	ICC practitioner
Abe M. Goff	1967	retired
Everett Hutchinson	1965	ICC practitioner
Howard Freas	1966	Southern Railway, assistant to president
Charles Webb	1967	Natl. Assoc. of Bus Operators, president
William H. Tucker	1967	Penn Central, vice president

Source: Robert Fellmeth, *The Interstate Commerce Commission* (New
York: Grossman Publishers, Inc., 1970), pp. 20–21.

it exists primarily to give jobs to its staff and to members of the industry it regulates, since the problems the ICC was set up to solve are no longer present. Railroads do not need to be protected from competition with other railroads because they are no longer engaged in cutthroat competition. ICC merger policy gave monopoly power to most companies in the industry long before the establishment of Amtrak, and before many of the transportation industries no longer needed protection from undercompetition. "In rate matters, the ICC acts only as an intermediary between carriers or, at best, between carriers and shippers. . . . Its main concern is to protect the economic position of the respective carriers—without regard to their efficiency."[11] Largely because of the existence of the ICC, it costs as much to move between Boston, Mass., and Champaign, Ill., as it does to move between Meridian, Miss., and Oakley, Kans., even though labor costs are lower in the latter case.[12]

THE WELFARE OF THE WEALTHY

Our laws distinguish between payments to the wealthy and payments to the poor. Welfare recipients must prove that they have tried to work, but some wealthy farmers are paid large sums for allowing their ground to lie fallow. "Clients" of some welfare agencies face a means test, while five grain exporters reap tens of millions of dollars in windfall agricultural subsidies. Under existing policies a man or woman who works to supplement his meager welfare payment is a "cheater" and can be struck from the rolls. Yet no one checks up on the many companies that are currently internalizing public wealth to see whether they are violating any government regulations. A handout to the wealthy is treated as a virtuous act; a payment to the poor is all too often regarded as an act of the devil.

A dual standard applies to many different aspects of our economic life. A doctor who manages to avoid reporting the fees he receives from Medicare patients is "shrewd." A loafer is subverting the basic attitudes of our society. An unconscion-

---

[11] *Robert Fellmeth,* The Interstate Commerce Commission *(New York: Grossman Publishers, Inc., 1970), p. 134.*
[12] *Fellmeth, p. 240.*

able housing operator who refurbishes old slums and sells them as new housing is "taking advantage of a good thing." An individual sitting at home and collecting his welfare check is immoral. It is an unfortunate truth of modern life that many sins are forgiven the gainfully employed that are not permitted to their less fortunate brothers.

Moreover, even among those who work, the system favors the wealthy. A person's title, as well as his output, seems to be the measure of his productivity. As Peter and Hull put it in their now classic *The Peter Principle*, "In our sophistication, we virtually shrug aside the immoral cleric, corrupt judge, incoherent attorney, author who cannot write, and English teacher who cannot spell."[13]

Old myths die a hard death. According to Wildavsky, a respected and hard driving Congressman insisted that poverty gives people its own incentive to overcome adversity.

> "I myself," he said, "would have been a lush if people paid
> me not to work." It was not enough to remind the legislators
> about the disincentives in the present welfare system, for
> they knew and objected already; their answer, however,
> was to suggest that the welfare system be made more
> unpleasant.[14]

The simple fact is that government agencies make many subsidy payments to the rich, both on an individual level and in the aggregate. Internalization of the public budget is more than a leisure time activity—it is a way of life for the warriors for wealth.

---

[13] *Laurence J. Peter and Raymond Hull,* The Peter Principle *(New York: William Morrow & Co., Inc., 1969), p. 4.*

[14] *Aaron Wildavsky,* The Revolt Against the Masses *(New York: Basic Books, Inc., Publishers, 1971), p. 74.*

6

TAXES AND THE SIMPLE MATHEMATICS OF WEALTH

*The tax laws, as drawn, appear to be a loaded
gun pointed at the rich and affluent.
But this is a tricky gun; as the ordinary man
pulls the trigger in high glee he shoots
himself! For the true muzzle of the weapon,
as in a fantastic spy film, points backward.*
—FERDINAND LUNDBERG

Looking back through the mists of time, it seems hard to believe that the American income tax began as a tax levied solely on the incomes of the wealthy. Before the Civil War, federal authorities relied on revenues from tariffs and from the sale of public lands to fill the coffers of government. As war approached, however, more and more men entered the army and Congress found itself forced to look for additional revenue to meet the growing costs of defense. Two potential sources looked extremely appealing: a tax on personal income and a tax on real property. After considerable discussion and debate, Congress enacted an income tax.

The first federal income tax was a tax on the wealthy because it applied only to people with incomes of $10,000 and over. The tax rates rose slightly with income (from 3 to 5 percent), and few exemptions were permitted. As time progressed, however, both the tax rates and the tax base increased. By the time the law was repealed (in 1872), the maximum tax rate had risen to 10 percent on incomes over $5,000.[1]

[1] B. Herber, Modern Public Finance (Homewood, Ill.: Richard D. Irwin, Inc., 1968), p. 205.

Once having tapped such a cornucopia of wealth, it was only a matter of time before Congress again enacted an income tax. It took a court ruling and the enactment of a constitutional amendment to obtain the right to tax income, but eventually the principle was established. The Tariff Act of 1913, like its predecessor, was aimed primarily at the incomes of the wealthy. Under the new law tax rates ranged from 1 percent (on family incomes of $4,000) to 7 percent (on incomes over $50,000). The income tax continued to be levied primarily on the incomes of the wealthy until World War II, when, in response to the rising costs of fighting the war, Congress reduced the number of exemptions in the law and increased the tax rate. For the first time the income tax became a major source of revenue, and it has been so ever since. In 1939, the income tax brought in about $1 billion. By 1970, revenues from the income tax had risen to $90 billion and constituted about 45 percent of the total taxes received by the federal government.[2]

As more income earners began to pay the income tax, the amount contributed by the wealthy became a smaller portion of the total revenue collected. When the rich were a major source of revenue to the government, any special concessions granted to them resulted in noticeably lower tax revenues. Once the income tax base was extended to include middle- and lower-income groups, however, it became easier for the rich to seek tax relief. Special concessions to them could be offset by small increases in the tax rates borne by the rest of the population. Alternatively, in good years the loss of revenue due to special concessions could be paid out of the revenue increases brought about by rising incomes. For the most part revisions in the tax code took place gradually, so that many Americans remained unaware of the concessions granted by the tax laws.

WELFARE PAYMENTS TO THE WEALTHY

Unknown to many people is a vast system of tax concessions to the wealthy. These take several forms. First, tax concessions are granted for the purchase of items that the government wants people to buy. For example, a taxpayer can deduct from

[2] *Joseph A. Pechman,* Federal Tax Policy *(New York: W. W. Norton & Company, Inc., 1971), p. 53.*

his income half the premium he pays on his medical insurance. Second, the government encourages the taxpayer to contribute to "worthy" causes such as public charities or private charitable foundations. Third, the taxpayer is permitted to deduct the expenses he incurs while doing business. Fourth, Congress provides direct tax relief to particular individuals. Through these and other devices, the tax laws provide considerable savings to the wealthy. At the same time, low- and middle-income taxpayers end up paying more taxes than they otherwise might. Whatever the government's motivation, be it as an agent of the warlords or as a misguided friend, it provides substantial subsidies to the rich through various provisions of the tax code.[3]

As a source of federal subsidies, the tax statutes are probably more efficient than the subsidy routes discussed in the last two chapters. There is no widely publicized and accepted national tax budget to alert the public to the special privileges provided by the tax laws, and no budget director weighs the benefits of each concession against its cost each year.[4] Once enacted, a tax preference is largely invisible and permanent, unaffected by "tight" budgets, economic conditions, and yearly budget reviews.

In view of the large number of tax concessions available to the rich, it is hardly surprising that for years a fortunate few paid no taxes at all. Table 10 shows the number of high incomes that escaped income taxation in 1961, 1966, and 1969. Note that tax-free returns rose dramatically in the late sixties, reflecting the increasing sophistication of the warlords, greater respect for the Treasury's ability to find unreported income,

[3] *Stanley Surrey, ex-assistant secretary of the treasury for tax policy, provides an alternative interpretation to that developed in this chapter and the following one: "The tax subsidies tumble into the law without supporting studies, being propelled instead by cliches, debating points, and scraps of data that are passed off as serious evidence. A tax system that is so vulnerable to this injection of extraneous, costly, and ill-considered expenditure programs is in a precarious state. . . ." U.S. Congress, Joint Economic Committee, "The Economics of Federal Subsidy Programs" (Washington, D.C.: U.S. Government Printing Office, January 1972), p. 49.*

[4] *It should be pointed out that the Joint Economic Committee requests such a budget from the Treasury each year. Nevertheless, this budget receives relatively little attention outside of Washington, and it is not incorporated in the President's budget.*

Table 10

NUMBER OF RETURNS THAT REPORTED NO TAXABLE
INCOME TO THE INTERNAL REVENUE SERVICE

| | Number of Nontaxable Returns | | | Percentage Increase, |
Adjusted Gross Income	1961	1966	1969	1961–1969
$1 million or more	17	18	52	305
$500,000 to $1 million	18	33	60	333
$200,000 to $500,000	42	103	188	448
$100,000 to $200,000	91	213	445	489
$50,000 to $100,000	284	617	1,479	521
$20,000 to $50,000	1,544	5,084	6,054	392

Source: U.S. Treasury, *Statistics of Income, 1961* (Washington, D.C.: U.S. Government Printing Office), pp. 20, 32; *1966,* p. 6; *1969,* p. 9.

and the greater number of returns reporting high incomes. It is a sobering thought to recall that until 1955 no Americans with incomes of $1 million or more were reported by the IRS as avoiding the income tax. And in 1955 only four millionaires reported paying no tax.[5]

Responding to the publicity given to these individuals, a high official from the executive branch told Congress that further analysis of the returns in excess of $200,000 revealed five principal causes of nontaxability: credits given for taxes paid to foreign governments, deductions for taxes paid to states and localities, charitable deductions, interest deductions, and deductions for miscellaneous purposes. The official went on to argue that the wealthy are paying federal taxes in large amounts and that the handful of returns showing nontaxable incomes represents a small proportion of those with high incomes.[6] Whatever the merits of his case, however, the public was clearly dissatisfied with the unfairness of the federal

[5] *Philip M. Stern,* The Great Treasury Raid *(New York: Random House, Inc., 1964), p. 8.*
[6] Tax Subsidies and Tax Reform, *Hearings Before the Joint Economic Committee, U.S. Congress (Washington, D.C.: U.S. Government Printing Office, July 1972), p. 157.*

income tax. And it is likely to remain so for many years to come.

In 1969, responding to the outraged cries of a public concerned about high taxes and tax cheaters, Congress enacted a series of tax reforms. One of these, the minimum-tax provision, attempted to ensure that all recipients of income pay at least some tax. This provision placed a 10 percent tax on income received from items receiving *preferential* treatment under the income tax. The term "preferential treatment" refers to the special concessions given to income from oil depletion, cattle raising, citrus groves, and other tax shelters. However, Congress stopped short of placing a minimum tax on *all* income. Individuals receiving income solely from state and local bonds, for example, continue to pay no federal income taxes under the new law.

How effective was the 1969 tax reform? IRS statistics for 1970 indicate that the minimum-tax provision cost 18,646 warriors for wealth nearly $117 million in taxes. But this is not the whole story. Although these taxpayers did pay some income tax, they paid at rates averaging a mere 4 percent! And the minimum tax did not even ensure that all persons with income over $30,000 paid at least some federal income tax. A total of 3,314 persons with incomes above $30,000 paid no income tax. Of these, 2,895 had incomes between $30,000 and $100,000, 394 reported incomes between $100,000 and $500,000, 22 had incomes between $500,000 and $1 million, and three had incomes over $1 million.[7]

In evaluating the success of the minimum-tax provision, Representative Henry Reuss said, "As things stand now, the minimum tax administers just a love pat to wealthy tax avoiders. They can continue to use tax loopholes if they will just pay a small admission fee for the privilege."[8]

Why are deductions and exemptions more valuable to the wealthy than to the poor? And which deductions are of special benefit to the wealthy? We shall answer these questions in the following sections.

[7] The New York Times, *March 27, 1972.*
[8] The New York Times, *March 27, 1972.*

ARE DEDUCTIONS AND EXEMPTIONS JUSTIFIED?

A person's income provides a fairly good indication of his ability to pay taxes. Nonetheless, adjustments must be made to reflect the fact that two people with equal gross incomes may not really have the same ability to pay. A person running a business of his own may incur certain expenses not required of white-collar workers or skilled craftsmen. He may, for example, be required to travel a great deal or to entertain prospective customers. In recognition of the fact that the expenditures required to conduct a business may not satisfy personal wants, some countries permit taxpayers to subtract some business expenses from their incomes.

Moreover, although two families may have equal incomes, they may differ in their personal circumstances. One family may have more children than the other, may be paying off past debts, or may have substantial medical expenses. The tax laws take these differences in ability to pay into account by permitting the taxpayer to deduct from income various personal expenses such as medical expenses, uninsured losses, and interest payments.

Also included are deductions for "worthy" causes like charities and charitable foundations. Deductions of this type are not based on ability-to-pay considerations but rather on the government's belief that socially desirable activities should be supported.

The government also permits taxpayers to claim personal exemptions. These exemptions apply to the taxpayer, his wife, and his children. As of 1973, for example, the taxpayer could claim $750 per person and additional exemptions if he was over 65 years of age and/or blind. Presumably the basic justification for these exemptions is that they remove from taxation the minimum income needed for subsistence. Together deductions and exemptions remove well over $20 billion in income from taxation under existing tax laws.

In theory, deductions and exemptions are necessary to ensure that people are treated fairly. In practice, they make the tax structure unfair by providing special treatment for the wealthy. Several things are responsible for this: (1) The mathematics of wealth are such that a deduction is worth more to a wealthy person than to a poor person. (2) Some provisions of the law provide concessions that the poor cannot take advantage of. For example, most middle-income families do not find it profitable to establish and contribute to charitable foundations, while many wealthy families do. Similarly, few middle-income families hold state and local bonds. Almost all of the bonds held by the public are in the hands of the wealthy. (3) Some provisions of the tax code deliberately provide special relief to wealthy individuals. Recall, for example, the Louis B. Mayer provision discussed in Chapter 4.

Figure 9 shows the difference between the rates scheduled under the tax law and the actual or so-called effective rates paid. Notice that the gap between the two rates increases with income. As income rises, some provisions of the tax code

Figure 9

INFLUENCE OF VARIOUS PROVISIONS ON EFFECTIVE
RATES OF FEDERAL INDIVIDUAL INCOME TAX, 1969 ACT[1]

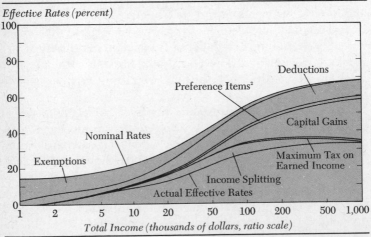

Source: Based upon Joseph A. Pechman, *Federal Tax Policy* (New York: W. W. Norton and Company, Inc., 1971), p. 69.

[1]Rates, exemptions, and other provisions of the Tax Reform Act of 1969 scheduled to apply to calendar year 1973 incomes.
[2]Preference items as defined by the Tax Reform Act of 1969, except excluded net long-term capital gains.

become more valuable. For example, income splitting (that is, filing separate returns for husband and wife) is useful to those families in the knight and warlord classes, while the capital gains provision is especially beneficial to the very rich. Although our statutory tax rates are progressive (that is, they rise with income), several provisions of the tax laws blunt the progressiveness of the tax schedule. On balance, the diagram suggests that the actual tax rates imposed on the *very* rich are *not* very different from the rates imposed on the estate class and the knights.

THE SIMPLE MATHEMATICS OF WEALTH

Deductions and exemptions introduce a personal element into the tax laws by recognizing differences in individual abilities to pay. Proponents of the existing system defend these on equity grounds. Why should a $10,000-a-year family with medical bills of $500 pay as much tax as a family with similar income but no medical bills? Doesn't the former have less ability to pay than the latter? And shouldn't a family experiencing loss from theft, fire, or severe storms be subject to some relief from the income tax? At first glance these arguments seem persuasive, but they obscure an elementary point. Although deductions appear to be justified on egalitarian grounds, they actually contribute to the inequality of the tax laws.

The mathematics of wealth operates in two ways. First, when a taxpayer takes a deduction of $1,000, the value of that deduction depends on his tax bracket. If he is in the 25 percent bracket the deduction is worth $250. In the 50 percent bracket it is worth $500. In other words, deductions and exemptions are worth less to the low-income than to the high-income taxpayer. Second, if the deduction or exemption is large enough, the taxpayer who takes it will pay at a lower tax rate than he otherwise would. This is because the rate at which a person's income is taxed depends on how much income he reports. With a taxable income of $30,000 a married taxpayer filing a joint return in 1971 might have paid $7,880, or 26.2 percent of his income, in taxes. If he succeeds in reducing his income to

$20,000, he pays only $4,380, or 22 percent of his reported income, in taxes. He saves $3,500. If there had been no change in his tax rate, he would have saved the $10,000 deduction multiplied by the average tax rate applied to $30,000 (26.2 percent, or a tax savings of only $2,620). Since the deduction changes his tax bracket, however, the taxpayer gains both the savings due to the deduction ($2,620), plus the benefit of having his remaining $20,000 taxed at a rate of 22 percent rather than 26 percent ($880).

In the following sections we shall consider only the direct value of deductions and exemptions. No attempt will be made to analyze the indirect savings attributable to a change in the taxpayer's tax bracket. To avoid other complications, we also assume that the taxpayers used in our examples find it more profitable to itemize their deductions than to take the standard deduction.

Personal Deductions: In Sickness and In Health

When a person becomes seriously ill, his ability to pay taxes diminishes. Taking this into account, Congress allows taxpayers to deduct a portion of their medical expenses. The law restricts the deduction to expenses totaling more than 3 percent of the taxpayer's income. This excludes minor medical bills and makes administration of the program easier. Nonetheless, this provision results in a $1.9 billion loss to the Treasury each year. A little arithmetic illustrates how the provision actually operates. Suppose that Snuff and Jones, two married men filing joint returns with their wives, both suffer from cancer. Snuff earns $5,000 and Jones earns $20,000. During the year each lays out $2,000 in medical expenses. When calculating his deductions, Snuff subtracts $150 (3 percent of his income) from his $2,000 in medical expenses, leaving $1,850 as a deductible expense. Jones subtracts $600, leaving $1,400 as a net deductible expense. Although the deduction for Jones is smaller than that for Snuff, Jones is in a higher tax bracket. Therefore, the deduction is worth more to him. The tax savings from claiming the medical deduction is $296 to Snuff and $392 to Jones. In other words, the medical deduction is worth almost $100 more to Jones than it is to Snuff, even though Jones is wealthier!

On July 21, 1972, Under Secretary of the Treasury Edwin S. Cohen testified before the Joint Economic Committee of Congress. The data he presented showed that the deduction for medical expenses was worth $470 million to taxpayers with incomes of $10,000–15,000 in 1971 and only $35 million to those with incomes of $100,000 or more. Thus the medical expense deduction appears to favor those with low incomes. But once the *number* of taxpayers in each group is taken into account, the medical deduction does not look nearly as egalitarian. The medical expense deduction was worth $33 *on the average* to taxpayers earning $10,000–15,000, while those taxpayers earning $100,000 or more claimed an average $449 worth of benefits.[9]

Almost all deductions are worth more to the wealthy than to the nonwealthy. This is because the value of the taxpayer's deduction depends on the income tax rate for the bracket in which his taxable income happens to fall. We can illustrate this point by examining what happens to the value of a taxpayer's deduction as his taxable income rises. Table 11 shows the value of a medical deduction—minus 3 percent of adjusted gross income—for several different income levels. Notice that, irrespective of the amount of medical expenses, the value of the medical deduction increases as taxable income increases.

Medical expenses can be devastating. Large bills rapidly

Table 11

THE MEDICAL DEDUCTION AND THE MATHEMATICS OF WEALTH*

Taxable Income	Value of a Medical Deduction of		
	$1,000	$2,000	$10,000
$ 3,000	$160	$ 220	$1,600
10,000	220	440	2,200
25,000	360	680	3,600
50,000	500	1,000	5,000

*Medical expenses are treated as net of the 3-percent-of-income deduction.

[9] Tax Subsidies and Tax Reform, *p. 216.*

deplete family savings and, in some instances, lead to debt. By permitting a tax deduction to families faced with major medical expenses, the government provides some tax relief. Over the years, however, this provision has favored the wealthy. What possible social goal is achieved by permitting a family with an adjusted gross income of $3,000 to reduce its tax by $160 on a $1,000 expenditure while a $50,000-a-year family saves $500 in taxes?

The 3 percent restriction does work in favor of people with low incomes and high expenses. Nonetheless, it does not offset the benefits of the medical deduction to the wealthy. For example, in theory low-income taxpayers may deduct such minor items as visits to an optometrist or a dentist from their income. But in many cases their total expenses do not exceed the 3 percent limit. Thus, this provision is usually not helpful to the poor. The rich are in a better position to purchase medical services, so they are probably the primary beneficiaries of the deduction, notwithstanding the 3 percent restriction. One eccentric old lady, for example, has an elevator in her house so that she can avoid the stairs. Since the elevator was recommended by her doctor, the expense is deductible. Another wealthy taxpayer takes frequent trips to Arizona to improve his health. The tax court has ruled that this is a legitimate medical expense. Although in some cases expenses of this type can be vital to a person's health, in others they merely serve to indulge the fancies of the well-to-do.

As a result of a recent liberalization of the medical deduction, people over 65 are now permitted to deduct all of their expenses without restriction. At first glance this seems laudatory, since older people are more likely to run up considerable medical bills than the young. Unfortunately, however, four-fifths of the elderly cannot take advantage of the new law— their incomes are so low that they do not pay any income tax.[10]

Personal Deductions: The Joys of Homeownership

Homeowners get special treatment under the federal tax laws. The homeowner who lives in a $30,000 house receives about

[10] *Stern, p. 209.*

$500 in untaxed income. If his house cost $75,000, his untaxed income might be about $1,350. The homeowner is an investor who chooses to take his return in the form of consumer services. To see this clearly, suppose that the homeowner decided to convert his return into real income. He could accomplish this simply by moving out of his house and charging rent to someone else. The tax laws would then treat that rent as income. If the owner lives in his own home, no tax is placed on the "implicit" income he receives.

By exempting this type of income from taxation, the tax laws provide an advantage to homeowners that is not shared by other taxpayers. And the laws do not stop here. They also permit homeowners to deduct state and local taxes paid on owner-occupied residences, as well as the interest on a home mortgage. These deductions are worth about $5.1 billion to homeowners each year. The interest deduction makes it cheaper for the person who cannot own a home outright to borrow money. It also discriminates between the person who has borrowed money to buy a home and the renter. These features of the tax law make homeownership attractive, especially for the wealthy.

Consider the following example, suggested by Philip Stern: Two families, the Failsafes and the Shortstops, each earn $10,000 per year and have $10,000 in savings. The Shortstops use all of their savings to make a down payment on a house. The Failsafes decide to rent an identical house from someone else and invest their savings in U.S. bonds yielding interest at 4 percent per year. Each year the Failsafes pay $2,000 in rent while the Shortstops pay $1,600 for mortgage, interest, maintenance, repairs, and insurance.

The tax laws permit the Shortstops to deduct from income the interest on their mortgage, as well as state and local taxes. Together these items add up to $1,000. Thus the Shortstops report a taxable income of $9,000 and pay taxes of $1,600. Because interest received on bonds other than tax-exempt state and local securities is taxable, however, the Failsafes report a taxable income of $10,400 and pay taxes of $1,908. Although the families are in almost identical circumstances, the tax laws discriminate in favor of the Shortstops.

At first glance the special treatment of homeowners does

not seem to be especially attractive to the wealthy. After all, many families that are not well-off own their own homes. But this impression fades when confronted by the facts. According to the *Federal Reserve Survey*, only 40 percent of the consumer units with incomes of less than $3,000 owned their own homes. Homeownership increased to 80 percent in the $10,000–15,000 income group, to 92 percent in the $25,000–50,000 group, and to 96 percent in the $100,000-and-above group. Thus the wealthy are more likely to benefit from the homeownership provision.

This is not the total story, though. People with higher incomes tend to have more expensive homes and to take a larger deduction than the poor. The mean value of a home in the under-$3,000 income group barely exceeded $3,200. (Recall that this figure is an average of all consumer units, including those with no homes.) In the $10,000–15,000 income group, the value of a home rose to slightly over $9,500, in the $25,000–50,000 group to about $32,500, and in the $100,000-or-more group to $88,200.[11]

While the middle-income taxpayer takes a $1,000 deduction on his tax return and rejoices in his gains, the warlord (or his accountant) deducts many thousands. In 1970, for example, out of the 18.1 million returns filed for incomes under $3,000, only 4.5 million (less than 25 percent) claimed any interest deduction, and the total amount claimed was 2.1 million. Of the 430,000 returns filed for incomes of $50,000 or more, almost 406,000, or over 94 percent, reported deductions for interest paid, and the total amount claimed was 2.4 billion.[12] Although the interest reported to the IRS includes all sorts of consumer purchases, a substantial portion of this amount is for home mortgage payments.

Personal Deductions:
Why It Is Better to Give Than to Receive

Contributions to religious, educational, and other nonprofit organizations are deductible under the income tax law. Over

[11] *Dorothy Projector and Gertrude Weiss,* Survey of Financial Characteristics of Consumers, *Federal Reserve Technical Papers, August 1966, p. 110. Hereafter referred to as* Federal Reserve Survey.

[12] *Internal Revenue Service,* Statistics of Income 1968 *(Washington, D.C.: U.S. Government Printing Office), pp. 6, 64.*

time the tax experts have found ways to make this type of deduction more attractive to the wealthy. A favorite method involves the donation of a long-held stock to charity. Suppose Piper buys 10,000 shares of Lonely Hearts Company and holds them for ten years. During this period the price of a share rises from $100 to $200, increasing Piper's wealth by $1 million. If he sells the stock he must declare a capital gain of $1 million and pay a capital gains tax of 35 percent, or $350,000, to the government. By donating the stock to charity, Piper avoids the capital gains tax completely. Since the record shows that he contributed $2 million to charity, he may then use his deduction to offset income from other sources.

The importance of this provision can be seen in Figure 10. The data show lifetime contributions to charity based on estate

Figure 10
LIFETIME CHARITABLE GIFT GIVING
BY SIZE OF ESTATE, 1957–1959

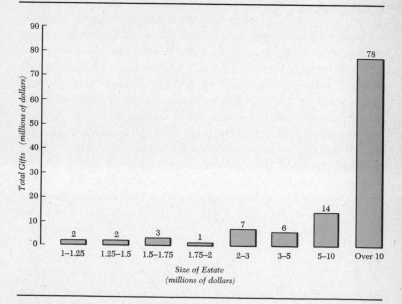

Source: Carl Shoup, *Federal Estate and Gift Taxes* (Washington, D.C.: The Brookings Institution, 1966), p. 180.

tax returns for 1957 and 1959. They clearly indicate that the very rich are generally the largest contributors to charity.

The tax loss from the charitable-deduction provision is enormous. Recent estimates suggest that religious, educational, and other nonprofit organizations cost the government almost $3.8 billion in revenue in 1970 alone. But proponents of this provision argue that charitable institutions perform a public service that the government would otherwise have to undertake. And the charities argue that they would have to close their doors if the government removed the tax deduction.

In addition to making contributions to public charities, taxpayers may deduct up to 20 percent of their income for contributions to private charitable foundations. Such organizations, discussed in Chapter 1, may be an important factor in contributing to industrial concentration. According to the Patman Committee, 111 foundations owned 10 percent or more of at least one type of stock in one or more of 263 different companies as of December 31, 1960.[13] By establishing a foundation, ostensibly to make contributions to charitable causes, an individual may maintain family control over his business without paying taxes. Such giants as Kaiser Industries (15.4 percent of common voting stock owned by the Emily and Ernest Woodruff Foundation), Eli Lilly & Co. (46.2 percent of common voting stock and 10.4 percent of class B nonvoting stock owned by Lilly Endowment, Inc.), and Kellogg Co. (58 percent of preferred nonvoting stock owned by W. K. Kellogg Foundation and 51 percent of common voting stock owned by W. K. Kellogg Foundation Trust) are closely linked to their founding families through the charitable-foundations provision.[14]

While some foundations have made a real attempt to make a charitable contribution, literally thousands of others are hidden behind a veil of secrecy. It is hard to avoid the impres-

[13] *Staff Report of the Subcommittee on Domestic Finance of the Committee of Banking and Currency, "Tax Exempt Foundations and Charitable Trusts" (Washington, D.C.: U.S. Government Printing Office, 1960)* p. 8.
[14] Ferdinand Lundberg, The Rich and the Super Rich *(New York: Bantam Books, Inc., 1969), p. 37.*

sion that many of these simply serve as vehicles for the internalization of wealth.

Other Personal Deductions

Several other deductions are permitted under the tax laws. These include casualty losses on property due to fire, theft, accident, and so on; interest payments for things like refrigerators, automobiles, and so on; and miscellaneous deductions for such items as losses for bad debts and alimony. Whereas these deductions benefit the wealthy more than other groups, their effect on the progressiveness of the tax system is not nearly as great as that of the items discussed earlier.

A BIRD IN THE HAND

Deductions and exemptions are relatively familiar to the average taxpayer. And perhaps more important, millions of taxpayers claim them each year. This works to the advantage of the very wealthy. Each time the issue of tax reform is raised, the warriors for wealth hasten to their various public platforms to decry the motives of the reformers. "Imagine the loss of the medical deduction!" "How cruel to thousands of elderly people." "What shall happen to the homeowner already overburdened by excessive property taxes if his deduction is removed, or to the household head trying to support six children if the $750 exemption disappears?" As soon as the word "reform" is heard in Congress, the alarm bell rings, and the public is warned, "Beware of the zeal of the reformers."

These tactics are very effective. Few members of the public understand the mathematics of wealth, and fewer still consider the cost of the subsidies provided to the very rich. The rich prevail precisely because they know how to appeal to the self-interest of others. Everyone knows that a deduction that one is sure of getting is better than a promise of lower taxes at some future date. So why should the $10,000-a-year wage earner support tax reform? The motto of the warriors for wealth rings out like a bell: "A little for a lot of people and a lot for just a few."

7
THE SHELTERED CLASS

In the affairs of the very rich, the tax rate table performs a poetic rather than a literal function. The mythic nature of the rate schedule for the rich was made quite clear when during the Kennedy Administration the maximum rate was reduced from 91 percent to 70 percent. There was at that time neither a deafening outcry from the Left nor a chorus of hosannas from the Right, for, politicians being practical men, it was recognized that nobody was actually obliged to pungle up all but 9 percent of his income.
— KENNETH LAMOTT

Personal deductions are an important source of inequities in the income tax law. Nonetheless, business-related deductions overshadow them. The tax laws offer special treatment to agricultural, manpower, housing, natural resource, and transportation activities. Deductions are also granted to taxpayers for various educational, international trade, and commercial development activities. These laws provide a potpourri of tax-reducing devices for people fortunate enough to qualify for them. In this chapter we examine several of these devices to show how they benefit the rich.

TRAVEL AND ENTERTAINMENT EXPENSES

Over the years the IRS and the courts have devoted considerable time to the question of what constitutes an acceptable business expense. Despite several attempts to reform existing rules, the travel and entertainment (T and E) deduction continues to provide a windfall of benefits to people with enough income to take advantage of it. The T and E deduction provides two forms of tax relief. First, it permits a taxpayer living away from home to deduct the cost of his transportation, meals, and lodgings, provided that he is on a business trip. Second, it enables a taxpayer to deduct the cost of entertaining his clients if the main purpose of the entertainment is related to business.

Under the 1913 Tariff Act businessmen could deduct "the necessary expenses actually paid in carrying on any business." In 1918 changes were made in the law that permitted a deduction for "all ordinary and necessary" expenses.[1] The vagueness of this phrase, together with the permissiveness of the IRS and the tax courts, has led to many questionable deductions. For example, one mortician deducted $77,700 from his income tax over a three-year period. This represented the costs of maintaining his personal residence, yacht, and guest cottage. When questioned about his rationale for deducting these items, he responded by claiming that they were necessary in order to entertain other morticians—an unusual way to increase business! Apparently the IRS partially accepted his rationale, for it allowed him to deduct $52,000 from his income tax.

Deductions of this type are quite common. Consider, for example, the wealthy manufacturer who transported his clients by company airplane to a company resort facility on a distant island. The manufacturer deducted almost $465,000 on his tax return. After an investigation the IRS permitted a deduction of almost $358,000.[2] Similarly, another firm was allowed about $112,000 toward maintenance of its yacht, $116,000 to run its ranch and hunting lodge, $126,200 to meet its nightclub expenses, and $119,000 for other entertainment.

At issue is the question of what is a necessary expense. Whether a particular trip, gift, or entertainment expense qualifies as a legitimate business expense depends largely on prevailing social attitudes. Until quite recently many Euro-

[1] *Philip M. Stern,* The Great Treasury Raid *(New York: Random House, Inc., 1964), p. 111.*
[2] *Stern, p. 111.*

pean and Asian business executives managed to conduct business without expensive evenings on the town. Most American businessmen did not. In Europe, contracts were signed and orders taken without the added inducements of a day at the football stadium or free tickets to a Broadway show. In America, many businessmen saw an evening's entertainment as a prerequisite for successful business dealings. Times change, however, and with the coming of age of multinational companies T and E expenditures are fast becoming an international custom.

Most Americans are at least vaguely aware of the T and E deduction. Interestingly, despite recent criticisms of the treatment of capital gains and oil depletion allowances, very little has been said about limiting T and E abuses. One reason for this is that many middle-income taxpayers take advantage of the T and E provision. Salesmen, manufacturers, lawyers, retailers, buyers, and doctors manage to charge an occasional dinner to Uncle Sam. Indeed, in some circles this is considered a mark of wisdom.

While many Americans see the T and E provision as beneficial, few recognize that the benefits they receive are a drop in the bucket compared to the tax-free expenses claimed by top executives, members of corporate boards of directors, and their assistants. Most Americans could pay lower taxes if the T and E provision were eliminated and replaced by the lower tax rates that could result if this and other loopholes were closed. Under a tax reform plan proposed by Benjamin Okner and Joseph A. Pechman of the Brookings Institution, for example, *average* tax rates might be cut by 42 percent.[3] And if T and E expenses are to be permitted as a tax deduction, the government might nonetheless recoup part of its loss by requiring the person who is entertained to report a portion of the entertainment on his income tax as a form of income in kind.

In 1961 President Kennedy laid before Congress a plan designed to curtail widespread expense account abuses. The President characterized the existing system as "a matter of national concern, affecting not only our public revenues, our

[3] *Benjamin Okner and Joseph A. Pechman, "Distribution of the Federal Income Tax by Income Classes." Paper presented at Southern Economic Association meeting, November 5, 1971, p. 20.*

sense of fairness, and our respect for the tax system, but our moral and business practices as well." His recommendations called for strict limits on the amounts deducted for entertainment, business gifts, and deductions for travel expenses. If enacted, they could have added $250 million to the Treasury's revenues.

Congress accepted a portion of President Kennedy's recommendations, making expenses for such items as yachts and hunting lodges nondeductible unless these items are used more than half the time for business purposes. It also required businessmen to itemize entertainment expenditures and to show that no substantial distractions precluded the conducting of business affairs. This provision appeared to close the door on visits to theaters, nightclubs, and sporting events. In fact, however, the legislators left the door open a crack by permitting taxpayers to deduct entertainment expenses if distracting events preceded or followed a business discussion. The new legislation also barred deductions for gifts to any one individual in excess of $25.

In tackling T and E abuses Congress failed to come to grips with many of the key issues. Most businesses would not need to entertain lavishly if the IRS made all entertainment expenses nondeductible. Similarly, the hardships created by closing the loopholes could be remedied. Some restaurants and nightclubs would close down. Many sporting events, Broadway theaters, and resort areas might also feel the pinch. But this is happening without tax reform. And the funds saved by taxpayers could be used to purchase other goods and services. Although some establishments might close, new jobs in other areas of the economy could fill the gap.

WHY BUSINESSMEN APPRECIATE DEPRECIATION

As indicated in Chapter 4, accelerated depreciation provides a means by which the government can encourage business investment. Under IRS rules firms are not permitted to deduct the full cost of capital equipment in the year in which the equipment is purchased. Instead, firms spread these costs out over the life of the capital asset. Several different methods are available for allocating costs, and some allow a larger allocation in early years than others. Businesses are not indifferent to the type of depreciation permitted by the government. The sooner a business can recoup its investment, the sooner it will have cash available to invest in other things.

Accelerated depreciation is attractive to businesses because it allows them to recoup their investment at a faster rate than would otherwise be possible. But the effects of this type of deduction are not all positive. For example, it favors firms expanding rapidly while offering little to those with no investment needs. In some industries, especially the housing industry, accelerated depreciation makes it profitable to turn over assets every few years. And in some cases firms may be encouraged to increase their investment even though they are producing at excess capacity! Finally, in most cases accelerated depreciation reduces the amount of tax received by the Treasury.

OIL DEPLETION AND THE DEPLETION OF THE FISC

One of the most blatant examples of favoritism in the tax laws involves the granting of liberal depletion allowances to the oil, gas, mining, and mineral industries. In his 1950 tax message, President Harry S. Truman said he knew of "no loophole so inequitable." Again in 1963, President Kennedy tried to plug this loophole but did not succeed.

The tax law permits firms engaged in extracting raw materials to take both a normal depreciation deduction and an annual depletion deduction. The effects of these tax concessions are substantial. In 1970, for example, all U.S. corporations paid an average tax of about 40 percent, while the large oil companies paid only 8.7 percent. Percentage depletion cost the government about $1.2 billion in 1970.

To appreciate how oil investment provides a high return to investors, consider the following example. Herbie Hopeful invests $500,000 in an oil exploration company, which uses these funds to drill a well. Approximately $100,000 of his investment goes into the purchase of heavy equipment like earth-moving machinery and pumps. The remaining $400,000 is invested in so-called intangibles, such as wages, fuel, and machine rentals.

If Herbie had invested his $500,000 in a nonextractive industry, the tax law would have required him to depreciate his capital investment over several years. Investment in the oil industry receives special treatment, however. Herbie can immediately deduct the $400,000 in intangibles from his tax return. The remaining $100,000 is subject to normal depreciation rules. As a result of this special treatment, he is able to reclaim 80 percent of his investment for immediate use elsewhere. In a nonextractive industry Herbie would reclaim his $400,000 investment over a period of years, foregoing the use of the funds until such time as they are returned to him. Of course, he must be wealthy enough to invest in oil—but after all, oil exploration is not a sport for the poor!

After the well begins to operate, the tax laws continue to discriminate in Herbie's favor. Congress permits him to keep 22 percent of his oil income or half his net profit (whichever is smaller) without declaring this on his income tax. For example, if the well produces an income of $50,000, he keeps $11,000 tax free. This allowance is defended on the ground that the draining of an oil well involves the depletion of a valuable resource of unknown value to the firm. The tax laws treat oil in the ground as a capital asset that eventually wears out.

In most instances the depletion allowance enables an investor to recover an amount far greater than his initial investment. In addition to permitting Herbie to deduct 80 percent of his costs and to depreciate the remaining 20 percent, it also grants him a 22 percent *yearly depletion* deduction. As long as the well produces income, he can continue to deduct 22 percent of his yearly oil income from his tax return. Since the deduction continues long after the initial capital investment is recaptured, the provision provides a substantial benefit to investors in the oil industry.

A 1960 Treasury Department study of six individuals with incomes of $1 million or more revealed that $3.8 million, or 46 percent, of the $8.3 million aggregate income of this group was offset by percentage depletion allowances on oil and gas, and $2.6 million was offset by deductions for intangible drilling expenses.[4] Three of the six millionaires paid no tax at all!

Special tax treatment for the oil industry became an issue after the 1913 Tariff Act. The amount deductible for tax purposes was initially limited to the original cost of the property. A series of changes led first to the use of the "fair market value" of the well at the time of discovery (an approach known as discovery depletion) and then, in 1926, to the use of percentage depletion. The Treasury estimates that these changes resulted in $985 million in foregone oil revenues in 1971 alone. Expenses of exploration and development added another $325 million to the lost revenues.

Since 1926, over 85 minerals have come under the percentage depletion provision. Congress currently permits percentage depletion allowances for such extractive items as china clay (15 percent), brick and tile clay (5 percent), gravel (5 percent), mollusk shells (5 percent), sand (5 percent), and slate (15 percent). Thus far no one has made a case for water, soil, or air. With environmental pollution becoming a major concern, however, special treatment for these supposedly inexhaustible items may not be far off. In fact, a recent court case granted a generous depletion allowance to a firm that used underground steam from nearby geysers to drive electric generators.[5] Pyramiding of special privileges is an important weapon in the war for wealth.

Oil has become an important source of wealth to people rising to the ranks of the very rich. A glance at Table 5 shows that over eight people at the top of the income distribution are involved in oil operations, including J. Paul Getty at the very top, as well as H. L. Hunt, James Abercrombie, and Jacob Blaustein. The presence of several oil-related names highlights the financial gains to those who are lucky and to those who learn to manipulate the tax laws for their own purposes.

What are the arguments for and against the depletion allowance? Advocates of the provision note the substantial risks associated with drilling a new well. In "wildcat" drilling eight out of nine tries turn out to be dry holes. A percentage

[4] *Joseph Ruskay and Richard Osserman,* Halfway to Tax Reform *(Bloomington: University of Indiana Press, 1970), p. 77.*

[5] *Ruskay and Osserman, p. 123.*

depletion allowance is necessary to raise the rate of return on oil high enough to encourage wildcatters to continue their activities. Moreover, once an oil well is discovered, each barrel extracted leaves one less in the ground.

Oilmen frequently take the position that the discovery of a new well involves the creation of new capital. The tax laws do not tax returns to capital in other industries, so why should oil be treated differently? They also argue that domestic exploration for wells is necessary for national defense. The United States must be able to provide its own oil supply in times of war, and this can be accomplished by encouraging companies to explore for new wells.

Critics of the depletion allowance emphasize the similarity between the oil taken out of the ground and a machine that depreciates. Both the oil well and the machine lose a portion of their value each year. And both are eventually worth very little to their owners. But the law treats these assets differently. The depreciation provision allows the owner of a machine to deduct the original cost of the machine over several years, while the oilman deducts his intangible costs immediately. Moreover, the oil depletion provision permits depletion deductions to continue until the well is dry, resulting in a deduction many times greater than the original cost. Why should the oil industry be treated any differently in this regard from other industries?

Critics also point out that drilling for oil is not nearly as risky a business as the oil companies would have one believe. Figures on business failures suggest that fewer oil companies go out of business than companies in other industries. Moreover, most of the depletion allowance does not go to the small wildcatters but rather to large oil companies. Stern notes that "In 1958 and 1959, out of every $100 in depletion deductions, about $70 went to the enormous companies that have assets of $100 million or more. Only the top 1/10 of 1 percent of American companies are that big."[6] Large companies tend to be cautious in their approach and to have a fairly successful drilling rate. In 1958, for example, the five largest oil companies drilled 3,447 productive wells and 868 dry ones. More-

6 Stern, p. 38.

over, these companies are in a better position to reduce risk by spreading it out over a large number of investments.

"Without government subsidy," the oilmen argue, "the return on oil exploration would be too low to yield the quantity of oil desired by the public." As a result, less oil would be marketed than is "desirable." But why should the private market take risk into account in other industries yet fail to do so in the oil industry? There is nothing inherent in the production process for oil that differentiates it from that of other marketable resources.

In fact, the subsidy to oil companies may cause an imbalance in the production process. As the rate of return from oil rises, more investors put their money into the oil companies. Therefore, relative to other industries there is an overinvestment of resources in the oil industry. The effect of this special treatment is to introduce a distortion into the resource allocation process and to generate an initial inequality of income in favor of people who can afford to invest in oil. Over time, however, the rate of return to oil drops as investors rush in to take advantage of the high return, and the rate of return to oil moves closer to that of other industries. But the net result of the tax laws is to encourage more investment in oil than would otherwise take place.

Those who favor the depletion allowance justify it as vital to the national defense. Said President Nixon, speaking in Texas in 1968, "I continue to believe that America's security requires the maintenance of the current oil depletion allowance." By subsidizing the oil industry through special tax provisions, the government encourages oilmen to search for more oil than they otherwise would. But critics of the allowance point out that it applies not to the *discovery* of the oil but rather to its *production*. Thus the subsidy is based on the using up of resources rather than on their conservation. This seems inconsistent with the view that the United States should encourage the conservation of a large supply of oil in case of war. Moreover, the extension of the depletion allowance to minerals other than oil and gas encourages producers to use virgin minerals instead of recycling existing resources. This seems to run counter to our ecological goals.

The year 1973 was a good one for the warriors for wealth. A shortage of heating fuel during the winter and of motor fuel in the summer gave a new argument to the depletion advocates. The American public was told that by increasing the depletion allowance they would make it profitable for the oil companies to discover new reserves, thus increasing the supply of oil. What the public was not told was that this short-run solution, although enormously profitable for the oil companies, would not meet the long-run energy needs of the nation. Instead, it would hasten the day when its reserves would be depleted. Moreover, the oil companies also failed to mention that they continued to export oil to other countries while complaining of shortages at home.

It is also hard to see how the present depletion provision is related to national defense, since it applies not only to oil produced at home but also to production in foreign countries. Indeed, over 40 percent of the depletion allowance goes to foreign producers. A subsidy to foreign oil operations would be meaningful if we wished to conserve our domestic oil for times of war. But from 1959 to 1973 Congress placed a quota on the amount of oil that could be imported from foreign countries, and this increased the amount of oil produced domestically. If the oil companies are to be singled out for special treatment, why not give a depletion allowance to all industries vital to the national defense? Perhaps the reason these industries are not included is that they already benefit through the subsidies suggested in chapters 4 and 5. Perhaps, too, they lack the political clout of the oil companies.

The effects of the depletion allowance and related provisions, such as the loss carryover provision, are clearly apparent when one examines the tax rates levied on the oil companies. The 1969 Reform Act reduced the oil depletion allowance from 27.5 percent to 22 percent. (It also made minor changes in the tax treatment of other mineral industries.) According to one source, this had little effect on Gulf Oil's federal tax rate, which rose from a meager 0.43 percent in 1969 to a bare 1.2 percent in 1970 and 2.3 percent in 1971. The tax rate is calculated by dividing the total tax paid by the company by net income after deductions are taken into account. Other oil companies actually had lower tax rates after the reform than before, as shown in Table 12. In 1970, for example, Texaco, Inc., had a tax rate of 6.4 percent; Standard Oil of California, 5 percent;

Table 12

FEDERAL TAX PAID AS A PERCENTAGE OF NET INCOME

Company	1969	1970	1971
Exxon Corp.	12.8	10.8	7.7
Texaco, Inc.	0.7	6.4	2.3
Gulf Oil	0.4	1.2	2.3
Mobil	5.7	10.9	7.4
Standard Oil of California	1.8	5.0	1.6
Standard Oil of Indiana	15.9	14.2	14.5
Shell Oil	1.7	12.4	14.9
Atlantic Richfield	1.5	4.1	3.8
Phillips Petroleum	13.6	10.0	15.0
Continental Oil	1.3	6.4	2.1
Tenneco, Inc.	*	13.3	NA
Sun Oil Co.	21.3	12.1	17.4
Cities Service	16.7	17.9	8.4
Union Oil of California	5.1	4.6	7.9
Amerada Hess	1.8	3.6	9.3
Getty Oil	8.1	21.9	15.1
Marathon Oil	1.9	5.3	6.1
Standard Oil (Ohio)	42.7	(10.4)**	2.0

NA—Not available.

*In 1969 Tenneco, Inc., reported a negative federal tax of $13,299. This gave it a negative tax payment of 14.3 percent.

**No explanation was given for the parentheses.

Source: "Oil Industry Paid 8.7 Percent in Federal Income Taxes in 1970," *Congressional Record*, 92d Cong., 1st Sess., vol. 117, no. 159 (October 27, 1971), S16896–16898. The 1971 figures are from *Parade* magazine, October 7, 1972, p. 17.

and Atlantic Richfield, 4.1 percent. In 1971, the tax rates were 2.3, 1.6, and 3.8 percent, respectively. (The tax rate depends on a set of factors including number of wells drilled, number of dry wells, and so on.) These rates compare favorably with those paid by corporations in other industries. By almost any standard, oil is a breeding ground for wealth.

CAPITAL GAINS: ASSET OR LIABILITY?

Capital gains and losses arise from the sale or exchange of capital assets. According to the Internal Revenue Code, all property qualifies for capital gains treatment except stock in trade or items held primarily for sale to customers in the ordinary course of trade, depreciable property, land used for business, copyrights, and certain other items. Since capital gains are taxed at a lower rate than ordinary income, enterprising warriors for wealth, together with the tax experts, have sought ways to stretch the definition of a capital gain to fit their needs. This effort has been quite successful. Stock option plans such as those noted in Chapter 2, "collapsible corporations," and a host of different schemes have developed over time. These help wipe out the distinction between ordinary income and capital gains.

In modern America the majority of capital assets are held by surprisingly few people. Recall that in 1962 approximately 1.4 million consumer units (that is, families and single individuals) with assets of $100,000 or more owned over 43 percent of the private wealth of the country and 65 percent of the nation's investment assets. Thus it is hardly surprising to learn that these families are the greatest beneficiaries of the capital gains provision. Out of 73.7 million tax returns filed in 1968, only 7.6 million listed capital gains. And according to the 1968 IRS *Statistics of Income*, those with adjusted gross incomes of $100,000–200,000 report 6.8 percent of the total capital gains, those with incomes of $200,000–500,000 report 6.4 percent, those with incomes of $500,000–1 million report 3.2 percent, and those with incomes of $1 million or more hold 5.8 percent of the total. Together, those reporting incomes of $100,000 or more hold over 22 percent of the total net reported capital gains. The relationship between the size of the taxpayer group and the percentage of capital gains reported by the group appears in Figure 11. It is interesting to note that the capital gains provision costs the Treasury about $5.6 million in foregone revenues from individuals each year.

Because the tax code places a premium on transforming ordinary income into capital gains income, it encourages individuals to distort their normal behavior patterns. Consider the hypothetical Elmer Campbell, a famous movie star, who owned an independent movie company. Instead of receiving a salary for his services, Elmer acquired a large equity in Campbell

Figure 11

PERCENTAGE OF NET CAPITAL GAINS HELD BY SELECTED
INCOME GROUPS IN 1968 BY ADJUSTED GROSS INCOME

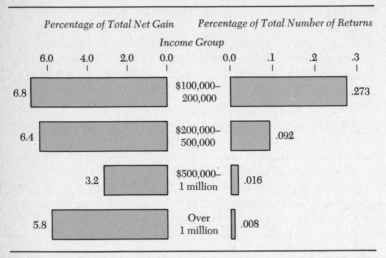

Source: Computed from Internal Revenue Service, *Statistics of Income 1968*
(Washington, D.C.: U.S. Government Printing Office), p. 34.

Limited. Because he succeeded in drawing masses of teenagers
to movie theaters, the value of Campbell Limited increased
considerably. He then converted his share in the company into
cash by liquidating equity holdings. His receipts were subject
to a maximum capital gains tax of 25 percent. Had he received
the income directly, the tax rate would have been substantially
higher.

Such distortions also occur in real life. Over the years such
stars as Tony Martin, Groucho Marx, Lucille Ball, Jackie
Gleason, and Sid Caesar have all established star-owned
corporations, primarily to reduce their tax bite.

The IRS recently cracked down on blatant abuses of this
type, but many less obvious loopholes persist. For example,
many highly successful corporations retain a portion of earnings instead of distributing them to shareholders. Since a tax
is levied on the increase in value of a capital asset only when
it is realized, the shareholders pay no tax on retained earnings.

But as a company's cash on hand increases, so does its net worth. This often results in an increase in the market value of the company's stock. A shareholder realizes a return on his investment by selling his shares. After paying the capital gains tax on the difference between the buying and selling price of the stock, he pockets the remainder.[7] Since dividends are taxed at ordinary rates while the appreciation in a stock's price is taxed at the capital gains rates at the time of sale, the shareholder saves on taxes by investing in companies that retain earnings. Of course this will work only if a stock's price rises over time.

Retained earnings are highly desirable to the wealthy taxpayer with no immediate need for dividend income. To illustrate why this is so, consider the following example. Suppose that two brothers, Herman and Steven Erp, both have investments. Herman own 10 shares of McTums hot dogs worth $10,000, and Steven invests $10,000 in Americana Furniture. At the end of year one, McTums retains its earnings increase of 10 percent, and this causes the value of Herman's shares to increase to $11,000. Steven receives $1,000 in dividends; after paying a 50 percent tax on them he reinvests in Americana, so his investment is now worth $10,500. In year two both stocks again yield a 10 percent return to their investors. Herman's stock's value rises to $12,100, an amount that is $1,075 greater than the value of Steven's stock. Each year the difference in the value of the two investments increases. A man wealthy enough to own stocks in companies that postpone payment of dividends may be able to establish a comfortable nest egg while avoiding the tax on dividends. This depends, of course, on a rise in the price of his shares.

Capital gains realized on the sale of a home also receive special treatment. An individual who sells his house and buys another within one year before or after the sale pays no tax on the appreciated value of his old house. If he sells his house and does not buy another within the time limit, the law requires that he pay taxes on the cumulative gain from all past resi-

---

[7] *Richard Goode*, The Individual Income Tax *(Washington, D.C.: Brookings Institution, 1964), p. 198.*

dences. The wealthy can use this provision to good advantage
by buying houses in several prime locations and holding onto
them while the properties appreciate. At the time of sale they
are taxed at capital gains rates.

Several types of income do not meet the requirements of a
capital asset but nonetheless receive capital gains treatment.
Suppose, for example, that Herman Erp owns an interest in an
iron mine. The royalties from this mine are not taxed as ordinary income. Instead, they are taxed at the capital gains rate.
Income received from the cutting and disposal of timber, coal
royalties, Christmas tree sales, livestock held for breeding or
dairy purposes, and the exercise of patent rights is also subject
to the capital gains tax rate.

Over the years various warriors for wealth have extended
the capital gains rate to a large number of products. We have
referred to this practice as the pyramid principle. Before 1964,
for example, coal royalties were treated as capital assets while
iron royalties were not. Coal owners achieved this privilege
by convincing Congress that their industry faced a hardship
situation. The lawmakers responded by granting capital gains
treatment to coal owners, even though no capital assets were
involved.

In 1963, the iron mine owners appealed to the congressional
sense of "fairness." Why should one type of mining operation
enjoy privileges not available to another? "After all," they
argued, "coal mines are not terribly different from iron mines."
Congress obligingly responded to their plea by extending
capital gains treatment to iron producers.[8] Similarly, Congress
granted special treatment to the timber industry. Shortly
thereafter the Christmas tree industry asked for and received
the same treatment. Under the *pyramid principle* warriors for
wealth use the gains made by some members of their ranks
to advance the cause of others. Once the first exception is made,
the rest follow.

Special treatment of capital gains is an historical by-product
of the war for wealth. The Tariff Act of 1913 treated such
gains as ordinary income. But the warriors for wealth did not
lie idle, and in 1921 the law was changed to permit taxation

[8] *Stern, pp. 84–85.*

of capital gains at a preferential rate. The treatment of these gains changed frequently during the 1920s and 1930s but remained stabilized after 1942. Under the provisions of the stabilized tax law, in force until 1969, half the capital gain on assets held for six months or more qualified for taxation at a rate not to exceed 25 percent.

In 1969 Congress paid its respects to the outraged taxpayer with a tip of the hat. To answer the demand for a fairer tax, capital gains above $50,000 were to be taxed at a 35 percent rate. Almost all of the other provisions of the capital gains law remained unchanged.

To appreciate the limited nature of the reform, consider the case of Mrs. Elder, who held 100 shares of Grant Motors for 40 years. During this period the stock's price rose from $5 a share to $500, and her initial holdings increased from a modest $500 to a comfortable $50,000. Mrs. Elder paid no tax on the appreciated value of the stock because it never changed hands. At her death her son inherited the stock, and shortly thereafter he sold all of the shares. The law states that when a stock is transferred at death the recipient need pay a capital gains tax only on any price appreciation that occurs *after* he becomes the owner of the stock. Since Mrs. Elder's son inherited the stock when it was worth $500 per share, he paid no tax on the price appreciation of $49,500. The rise in the initial price of the stock from $5 to $500 per share escaped taxation completely! Elderly taxpayers frequently prefer to avoid taxation of capital gains by holding their stocks until death. The experts refer to this phenomenon as a "lock-in" effect. Richard Goode explains that

> Certain switches that will increase the earning power of an investor's portfolio will nonetheless reduce the size of his estate. For example, a switch that is fully justified by rate-of-return calculations will reduce an investor's estate if it involves the payment of a substantial capital gains tax and the investor dies shortly thereafter.[9]

In other words, the tax laws may make it unprofitable for investors to switch from one stock to another, even when a

[9] *Goode, p. 210.*

switch would otherwise be profitable. Despite the widespread cries for reform, Congress chose to avoid a provision requiring realization of capital gains at death.

The special treatment provided by the capital gains law could be limited in several ways: (1) The time that individuals must hold a stock in order to qualify for long-term capital gains could be extended from six months to twelve months. This would eliminate some of the short-term speculation in the stock market. (2) Long-term capital gains privileges for special industries such as timber cutting and oil and coal mining could be withdrawn. This action would simply recognize that industries do not really meet the capital gains definition discussed earlier. (3) Congress could adopt the principle of constructive realization of gains at death (current laws permit indefinite deferral of the tax). Under this proposal a tax would be placed on the appreciated value of a stock whenever the owner of the stock died. (4) Capital gains income could be taxed at the same rate as ordinary income. Although this might cause some transitional problems, they would be temporary.

Special treatment of capital gains is one of the pillars of the war for wealth. It is selective, obscured from the public view, and sanctioned by time-honored tradition. By eliminating the special rates for capital gains, Congress could go a long way toward achieving a fairer distribution of income. But as long as the warriors for wealth maintain their stolid defense of the status quo, elimination of this provision remains unlikely.

HOW TO BUILD A REAL ESTATE WITH REAL ESTATE

According to one author, "Ever since the early American settlers bought land for two cents an acre, real estate has provided the largest single means to the accumulation of individual fortunes in this country."[10] He lists the following benefits of real estate:

---

[10] *Daniel J. de Benedictis,* The Complete Real Estate Advisor *(New York: Pocket Books, 1970), p. 169.*

1. Greatest net cash return on your actual investment. Investment buyers normally demand 10 to 15 percent per year minimum clear net profit on their actual cash investment . . .
2. Amortization—the total principal savings per year on all the mortgage payments you make, using your tenant's money.
3. Depreciation—usually 3 to 5 percent each year on the total investment. This tax deduction, allowed on all income property, acts as a very profitable offset to your income tax liability.
4. Appreciation—the ever increasing value of most income property through general inflation . . .
5. The availability of the minimum 25 percent capital gains tax (now 35 percent on gains of more than $50,000) so long as you hold the property at least six months (now about 7 years).
6. The extra increase in value obtainable by buying in a growing area . . .[11]

In few other areas are the tax laws so in accord with the wishes of the investor. A shrewd operator buys a new building, depreciates it rapidly, and uses the tax advantage he receives to offset his income from this property. As long as inflation occurs, he is able to sell his property at a higher price and take the profits resulting from a higher price as capital gains.

Consider the following example, based on an earlier version by Stern. Robert Hughes, a wealthy real-estate tycoon, constructs a new $5 million apartment building, the Towers. Each years Hughes nets $200,000 in cash from the Towers' tenants. In the first year Hughes also claims a depreciation deduction of $250,000, which he uses to offset the $200,000 in rental income. The remaining $50,000 is used to offset income from other sources. Since Hughes is in the 70 percent bracket, his tax savings are $175,000 in the first year and $875,000 in the first five years of the building's life.

Twelve years after the Towers is constructed, Hughes accepts an offer to buy. By now he has taken tax deductions of about $3 million, and the book value of the building has been reduced to $2 million. The purchaser offers him $6 million for

[11] *De Benedictis, p. 170.*

the property, and Hughes willingly accepts. By doing so he realizes a substantial return on his investment. While he owned the building Hughes saved 70 cents on every dollar that he claimed for depreciation. And now that he intends to sell, Uncle Sam sweetens his investment still more. After subtracting the depreciated book value ($2 million) from the selling price of the building ($6 million), Hughes shows a profit of $4 million. Since this profit is treated as capital gains income, he pays only $1.4 million (35 percent of the $4 million) in tax.

Hughes has depreciated the building on his tax returns during the first few years. By selling the Towers and buying a new building, he can again claim substantial depreciation deductions. Moreover, the purchaser of the Towers may begin depreciating the building again, this time on the basis of a $6 million purchasing price. The process can go on indefinitely, although the law now limits rapid write-offs for buyers of used buildings.

Accelerated depreciation is especially favorable to investment in real estate. The rapid write-off allowed by the Treasury is not related to what is actually happening to the property. Accelerated depreciation presumably reflects the rapid wearing out of the property. In recent markets, however, property like the Towers does not depreciate quickly. While the building may be depreciating, the land on which it stands is appreciating, thanks to inflation. Thus, accelerated depreciation is based on a fiction. Investors who take advantage of this provision can not only write off substantial sums during the first few years that they own a property but also count on substantial price appreciation as well.

By selling his property at a time when he can take a capital gain on the difference between the price he receives and the depreciated book value, the investor gets the best of both worlds. As long as there is an asymmetry between the tax rate levied on ordinary income (70 percent in this example) and the rate at which capital gains are taxed (35 percent), this difference will provide a margin of profit for the investor. And as long as he is willing to buy and sell every few years, he can stay ahead of the Treasury.

The Kennedy administration proposed two measures designed to eliminate some of the special advantages enjoyed by real-estate owners. The first called for elimination of "fast depreciation" in favor of "straight-line depreciation." The second attempted to eliminate taxation of the difference between the selling price and the depreciated value of the property at the capital gains rate rather than at ordinary rates. In 1962 Congress took steps to limit the capital gains treatment of personal property, but it refused to modify the law dealing with real estate. The Kennedy administration then sought to modify its proposal by introducing a sliding scale that lengthened the time a building must be held before it is eligible for full capital gains treatment to 15 years. But even this modification aroused the ire of the warriors for wealth, and the proposal failed to clear the House.[12]

Under the Tax Reform Act of 1969, most investors are barred from using such extreme accounting practices as double-declining-balance and sum-of-the-years-digits. Some limits are placed on the extent of the capital gain that can be taken on a depreciated building. Yet the new reforms fail to eliminate the multiple advantages received by investors in real estate.[13] A recent Treasury estimate suggests that depreciation on buildings (other than rental housing) in excess of straight line results in a $480 million loss to the government each year. Including rental housing increases the estimate by another $500 million.

STATE AND LOCAL BONDS—ACHILLES' HEEL

Since the income tax of 1913 was enacted, interest earned on state and local bonds has been exempt from federal taxation. The amount of state and local debt outstanding has risen rapidly—from $5.3 billion in 1950 to $18.5 billion in 1960 and $35.7 billion in 1968.[14] The large supply of such bonds provides a wide range of alternative investments for people who want to obtain their income in a tax-free form.

Surprisingly little information is available on the purchasers of state and local bonds. According to the 1962 *Federal Reserve*

[12] *Stern, pp. 153, 155.*
[13] *Ruskay and Osserman, p. 177.*
[14] *U.S. Bureau of the Census,* Statistical Abstract of the United States 1970 *(Washington, D.C.: U.S. Government Printing Office), p. 417.*

Survey, a negligible number of consumer units with assets under $50,000 own state and local bonds. About 3 percent of those in the $50,000–100,000 group and 2 percent of all units with incomes between $100,000 and $200,000 owned bonds of this type. The percentage increased with wealth—to 15 percent in the $200,000–500,000 group and 41 percent in the $500,000-and-over group. On the average those in the first asset group owned $308 worth of such bonds, in the second group $147, in the third $1,920, and in the last $51,721. (Recall that these figures represent an average for both owners and nonowners of such bonds.)

The importance of these ownership patterns is dramatically brought out in the figures presented by Under Secretary of the Treasury Edwin S. Cohen to the Joint Economic Committee in 1972. According to Cohen's figures, those with adjusted gross incomes of less than $3,000 receive an average 28 cents in tax benefits as a result of the exemption of state and local interest. Families in the $10,000–15,000 income group receive an average tax subsidy of 71 cents, while the figure increases to $27.81 for the $20,000–50,000 income group and to about $853.00 in the $50,000–100,000 income group. However, for those with incomes of $100,000 or over the average tax benefit from the state-local bond interest deduction is over $4,620.[15]

Because of their tax-free status, state and local securities provide a greater return to the rich than to the poor.[16] A person who can invest $2 million in tax-free bonds, for example, may receive $100,000–140,000 a year of tax-free income. As a result almost all of the state and local bonds in the hands of the public are owned by people with high incomes. The rest are owned by banks and insurance companies. To see why these bonds are attractive to the wealthy, consider the value of a 3 percent tax-free bond. A taxpayer in the 10 percent tax bracket must receive 3.3 percent interest on a taxable bond in order to secure the same 3 percent return after taxes. In the 30 percent bracket, the taxpayer must receive a 4.3 percent return in order to earn 3 percent on a taxable security; in the 50

[15] *Tax Subsidies and Tax Reform, Hearings Before the Joint Economic Committee (Washington, D.C.: U.S. Government Printing Office, July 1972), p. 213.*
[16] *Municipals must usually be bought in $1,000 or $5,000 denominations, making them difficult for the poor man to afford.*

percent bracket, he must receive 6 percent; in the 60 percent bracket, he must receive 7.5 percent; and in the 70 percent bracket, he must receive 10 percent. Thus tax-free bonds are worth more to the wealthy.

Since the interest rate for state and local bonds is determined in the marketplace, the increased demand for such bonds—resulting from their tax-free status—tends to drive their interest rate down. If investors act rationally they will continue to purchase tax-exempts until there is no difference between the net return received on tax-exempts and that on nonexempts. And as the demand for tax-exempts rises relative to the demand for nonexempts, a difference will arise in the interest rates of the two securities. This represents the amount of gross interest the investor is willing to forego in order to gain a tax advantage. But if the supply of tax-exempts rises more rapidly than the demand, the interest rate differential may be small compared to the tax advantage. This appears to have happened during the last decade as many communities sought to keep pace with ever-rising costs through the issuance of tax-free bonds.

From the borrower's (state or local government's) point of view, the lower interest rate on state and local securities is a subsidy from the federal government that enables it to borrow at a lower interest rate. From the wealthy bondholder's perspective, the lower interest rate may be more than offset by the potential tax reduction. And from the government's point of view, the subsidy program costs the taxpayer over $2.6 billion each year![17]

State and local securities offer other attractions. They are essentially risk free, since the principal is secured by the taxing power of the community.[18] A ready market exists for their purchase and sale, and they are fairly liquid. Moreover, the major bond-rating services provide fairly extensive information on their financial characteristics.

Among the strongest proponents of the tax-exempt status of these securities are state and local government officials. During the hearings on the 1969 Tax Reform Act, many officials argued

[17] *Tax Subsidies and Tax Reform, p. 164.*
[18] *However, this is true only of general obligation bonds. Revenue bonds are not secured by a community's tax power.*

that without this provision state and local governments would have to pay substantially higher interest rates to investors. Several alternatives to the present system also failed to please them. For example, federal subsidy of the interest rate was rejected as a type of financing that would threaten their independence. Many also argued that a federal tax on these bonds would violate the Constitution.

The current method of subsidizing the states (and coincidentally, the wealthy) is strange for several reasons. Empirical studies suggest that the savings that state and local governments receive by virtue of their tax-exempt status are only half as great as the revenue the federal government loses by this provision. Moreover, the benefits to a state depend on how much it borrows. In fact, the more it borrows the greater the subsidy it receives! Thus the states with the greatest debts receive the largest subsidies. Finally, the advent of revenue sharing may lessen the need for this type of aid.

During the push for reforms in 1969, Congress considered and rejected a proposal to change the tax status of state and local bonds. As formulated, the proposal applied only to new securities; it would not have affected the tax-free status of existing state and local bonds. This proposal failed to be included in the final bill. Congress did pass a minimum tax designed to obtain at least some taxes from wealthy individuals who had previously escaped taxation on all or most of their income, but state and local bond interest was not included as taxable income. Because of this exclusion, as well as others, more than 3,300 people who earned over $30,000 paid no federal income tax in 1970.

EVOLUTION OR REVOLUTION?

The 1969 Tax Reform Act was designed to alleviate broad-based voter dissatisfaction with the existing tax structure. But the widespread discontent that gave rise to these reforms remains. A 1971 poll by Lou Harris showed that 69 percent of the public sympathized with a taxpayer revolt. And in mid-1972 the presidential candidates again found themselves talking about tax reform.

Each year more Americans seek ways of reducing their taxes. Many have turned to professional tax services. In 1972, for example, the Internal Revenue Service found that 95 percent of the tax returns made out by "professional tax services" showed fraudulent deductions or exemptions. In their rush to take advantage of all the deductions they can, American tax-payers have discovered a large number of exotic deductions that they are unable to take. Perhaps as a result, many tax-payers claim deductions to which they are not entitled. Increasingly they have made their feelings known about the special benefits the wealthy receive.

Our existing tax laws must change if the income tax is to survive as a viable source of revenue. If the American public were to decide to stymie the tax collectors, it could easily do so. As Randolph Thrower, former commissioner of the Internal Revenue Service, told Congress, "In view of the declining enforcement a well directed challenge to federal taxes could prove costly and disruptive to our tax system. . . ."[19]

In 1969, outgoing Secretary of the Treasury Joseph A. Barr spoke of a taxpayer revolt not from the poor but from the middle class, who are outraged at "high income recipients who pay little or no federal income tax."[20] Although it is unlikely that Congress will remove all of the provisions favorable to the rich, some patently unfair provisions, such as the oil depletion allowance, will eventually have to go. For unless Congress pays greater attention to the needs of the middle-income tax-payer and to the poor, the taxpayer revolt may give way to a taxpayer revolution.

[19] The Wall Street Journal, *January 19, 1969.*
[20] The Wall Street Journal, *January 20, 1969.*

8
TO THE CREDIT OF THE WEALTHY

*One wonders, inevitably, about the tensions
associated with debt creation on such a
massive scale. The legacy of wants, which are
themselves inspired, are the bills which
descend like the winter snow on those who are
buying on the installment plan. By millions of hearths throughout the land it is
known that when these harbingers arrive the
repossession man cannot be far behind.
Can the bill collector be the central figure
in the good society?*
—JOHN KENNETH GALBRAITH

Millions of Americans await
their weekly paychecks with moderated enthusiasm. For after
deducting payments to the finance company and other credit
institutions, the average family has little to look forward to.
In 1971, for example, outstanding consumer credit exceeded
$137.2 billion. The public spent almost $110 billion for installment loans (that is, loans paid back gradually over a period
of time) and over $2.7 billion more for noninstallment loans.[1]
These figures imply an average debt of $666 for every man,
woman, and child in the United States. Focusing solely on
installment debt, the *1970 Survey of Consumer Finance* found
that almost *half* of the families surveyed had debts outstanding.[2]

[1] Federal Reserve Bulletin, *May 1972, 56.*
[2] *George Katona*, 1970 Survey of Consumer Finance *(Ann Arbor, Mich.:
Braun-Brumfield, Inc., 1971) p. 22.*

148

At first glance one might expect to find the rich in the business of lending rather than borrowing. After all, cross-section studies of consumer spending have found that the amount a family saves (and therefore has available to make loans) increases with its income. Moreover, the figures presented in Chapter 1 show that the nation's private wealth lies in the hands of a select few. Recall that in 1962 about 2 percent of the consumer units owned over 43 percent of the private wealth and 65 percent of the investments in the United States.

Nonetheless, many wealthy people are borrowers. In 1966 over 2.9 million taxpayers with incomes over $15,000 reported interest paid on personal debts, mortgages, and other forms of consumer credit. Among taxpayers in the $1 million-and-above group, over 78 percent of those who itemized deductions listed an average of $68,800 in deductible interest payments. Similarly, over 73 percent of those in the $200,000-500,000 income group reported deductible interest payments.[3] The IRS data, like those compiled by the Federal Reserve, suggest that the wealthy incur debts.

Why do the well-to-do borrow money when they seem to have sufficient funds to cover their needs? Does the capital market operate so as to reinforce the effects of the war for wealth? And what other forces are at work? These questions will be explored in this chapter.

BORROWING: THE NEED AND THE NEEDY

Paradoxically, our credit institutions provide the cheapest forms of credit to people with high incomes and a stable home environment. Those with a set of qualifications that meet the standards of a local credit bureau can usually obtain credit from a bank or credit card company at simple interest rates ranging from 9 to about 18 percent. People without such qualifications, primarily the poor, are left to the mercy of small, costly finance companies or disreputable loan sharks. These unfortunate castouts pay interest rates ranging from 25 to 300 percent or even more.

[3] *Internal Revenue Service,* Statistics of Income, 1966 *(Washington, D.C.: U.S. Government Printing Office), p. 60.*

Figure 12 shows the various types of loans made to consumers. Real-estate mortgages and borrowings against insurance policies are excluded from the analysis. Notice that
automobile installment loans account for the largest portion
of consumer credit, amounting to over $38.3 billion, or 28 per-
cent of the total, in 1971. Personal installment loans for such
purposes as consolidation of consumer debts, payment of taxes
and insurance premiums, travel, and education expenditures
account for $34.4 billion. Other consumer loans for goods like
home appliances, furniture, and jewelry amount to $32.4
billion. In contrast to these, loans for repair and modernization
and charge account loans barely compare in importance.
Single-purpose noninstallment loans, made directly to consumers, and credit loans, consisting primarily of amounts owed
by consumers to professional practitioners and service establishments, constitute a small share of total consumer credit.

Figure 12
TOTAL CONSUMER CREDIT, 1971

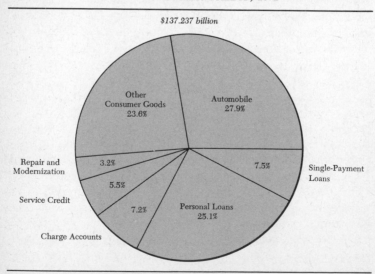

What credit sources are available to an individual with a good credit rating? Suppose that a $10,000-a-year office worker, Henry Hawkins, decides to finance a new $600 color TV by spreading out his payments over the life of the set. Because he has a good credit rating, Hawkins may take out a loan from several sources, including (1) the commercial-loan department of a local bank, (2) the installment-loan department of the same bank, (3) one of several bank credit card companies, (4) a credit union, (5) the dealer who sells the color TV, (6) one of several small- or medium-sized loan finance companies, and (7) a local loan shark or a so-called "juice racketeer."

Many banks have two types of loan departments—commercial and installment. Although the former are best known for their business loans, some will lend funds directly to consumers. In fact, by borrowing from a commercial-loan department Hawkins may be able to obtain highly favorable terms. For example, commercial-loan departments seldom levy a penalty if a loan is repaid early. Moreover, they feel the effects of favorable national credit policies almost immediately: When the prime interest rate drops, the first borrowers to benefit are those making commercial loans. And although the interest paid on commercial loans is not inconsequential (small borrowers usually pay interest at rates between 9 and 10 percent), it is lower than that charged for an installment loan. On an installment loan the finance charge is deducted before the customer gets the money. Thus the "real" interest rate works out to be about 18 percent.[4]

To qualify for a loan from sources (1)–(3), Hawkins must possess a good credit rating based, in part, on demonstrated ability to repay a loan when it is due. The key to his credit rating is the credit dossier kept on file at one of over 2,500 credit bureaus located throughout the United States.[5] Anyone who has ever charged a purchase at a local store, borrowed money, had a telephone installed in his home, or paid an electric bill is likely to be listed in a credit bureau file. The

[4] *Al Griffin*, The Credit Jungle *(Chicago: Henry Regnery Co., 1971)*, *pp. 197–198.*
[5] *Griffin, p. 154.*

rating assigned by this bureau affects the willingness of a vast array of institutions—ranging from the local bank to the nearby supermarket—to issue credit. Together, these institutions determine the terms on which credit is extended to an individual.

A poor credit rating raises Hawkins' cost of obtaining funds substantially. According to Griffin,

> The people who can least afford legally high interest rates
> are the ones who borrow money where it costs the most:
> through personal loan companies. They are indeed licensed,
> but what they have is a license to steal. Interest rates start
> at 24 to 30 percent—and go up. A flat 3.5 percent per
> month is the going rate on many small loans: that's 42
> percent a year.[6]

Moreover, small-loan companies begin to pressure the borrower to pay up almost from the day he takes out a loan. Should he default or procrastinate with his payments, such outfits are not above the use of brute force. Although Griffin may overstate the profits of small-loan companies, his analysis of their practices is quite sound.

In his book *Buy Now Pay Later*, Hillel Black illustrates what it is like to deal with a small-loan company:

> The gunman entered the small loan office, pulled out a
> revolver, aimed it at the girl at the reception desk, and
> said "Put the money in this paper bag." The girl looked at
> him with the coldest blue eyes you ever saw and snapped
> "You can't have it. It's against company policy." There was
> only one thing the gunman could do. He turned and fled.[7]

Even if Hawkins receives a poor credit rating, he may still be fortunate enough to qualify for a low-cost loan from a credit union. A credit union is a group of people who have joined forces both to save and to make loans to each other at low interest rates. Credit unions commonly arise in companies,

---

[6] *Griffin*, p. 207.
[7] *Hillel Black*, Buy Now Pay Later *(New York: Cardinal and Company, 1961), p. 149.*

churches, fraternal organizations, and labor unions or among people living in the same neighborhood. They grant loans on the basis of a borrower's character rather than his credit rating. Most charge an interest rate of 1 percent per month on the outstanding balance of a loan—an amount equal to a simple interest rate of 12 percent per year.

Although over 23,700 credit unions in the United States served over 22.8 million members in 1970, they provided relatively little assistance to the poor. In a survey of its clientele, the Credit Union National Association found that only 4 percent of all credit union families had incomes below $5,000. Nearly two-thirds had incomes above $10,000, and 36 percent had incomes between $10,000 and $15,000.[8]

Of course, Hawkins might finance a color TV by borrowing directly from the store at which he makes his purchase. Many retail dealers, especially in the boating and appliance industries, will make conditional sales arrangements like those offered by automobile dealers. These contracts provide that the lender shall hold title to the merchandise until the borrower pays off the full value of his loan. Under this stipulation, if the borrower misses his monthly payments the lender may repossess the merchandise without refunding the amount previously paid in. Changes in the law now restrict the terms under which credit merchandise can be repossessed, introducing an element of fairness long overdue in the credit market. For example, in New York the law protects the borrower in that if a certain amount has been paid toward the purchase of an item, that item must be offered for public sale. After payment of his debt the borrower receives the amount left over.

To ensure that a loan is profitable, dealers in such items as boats and snowmobiles sometimes charge interest rates averaging 22 percent or more. Most dealers work with "cooperating" lenders who share their profits with the dealers, using such devices as kickbacks and commissions on the life insurance policies that borrowers must take out to cover the loan in the event of death.[9]

---

[8] Credit Union Yearbook, *1971, pp. 25–26.*
[9] *Griffin, pp. 83–84.*

Credit provided by dealers plays an important role in facilitating automobile purchases. According to the annual report of General Motors Acceptance Corp. (GMAC), over $7.2 billion worth of retail credit contracts were held by GMAC throughout the world in 1971. GMAC funds financed almost 3.9 million retail contracts, of which 2,438,000 were for new cars, 1,249,000 financed used cars, and 174,000 covered various other products (primarily household appliances). Of the 12.3 million new cars sold in the United States in 1971, including imports, GMAC credit financed almost 20 percent! And over the life of his car (32.7 months), the average purchaser of a GMAC contract laid out $115 each month, paying a total of $3,760 in purchase price plus interest.[10]

Available evidence suggests that despite their willingness to assume greater risks, small-loan companies reject about 50 percent of their applicants.[11] Those rejected have little recourse but to borrow from a loan shark or a juice racketeer. A juice racketeer gets his name from his practices. The "juice" refers to the extremely high interest payments he receives. These unregulated and often illegal birds of prey are not concerned with repayment of a loan but rather with prompt receipt of monthly payments.

Loan sharks and juice racketeers are fairly common in several states. Writing in 1961, Black argued:

> The scourge in Texas has reached such huge proportions
> that it is doubtful that any state has supported as many
> credit swindlers or debtor victims. Until recently cursed by
> an unworkable usury provision in its constitution that
> limited interest rates to 10 percent a year, Texas could make
> the dubious claim of maintaining a loan shark industry with
> annual volume of about three hundred million dollars.
> In fact, the operation is so vast that the loan sharks for
> descriptive purposes must be divided into two groups.
> One group, the small small-loan companies number between
> one thousand and fourteen hundred . . . (for this group)
> the interest rate annually starts at 220 percent. Though the

[10] *General Motors Acceptance Corp.*, Annual Report, 1971.
[11] *Black, p. 175.*

second group numbers only 275, their annual volume ranges
as high as $250 million. They deal almost exclusively in
secured loans of between $100 and $3,000. Their effective
interest rate ranges from 35 to 80 percent.[12]

Despite legislative changes to outlaw the worst practices of
loan sharks, their grip has not diminished over time. Instead,
their practices have taken a slightly different form. In a 1963
study, *The Poor Pay More*, David Caplovitz reported that
several of the families in his study patronized loan sharks,
while many more were victimized by usurious door-to-door
salesmen.[13] These unconscionable operators capitalized on the
loneliness and isolation of the poor to sell them shoddy goods
at ridiculously high prices. And in 1971 Griffin discussed
several cases of usury, including that of an Ohio operator who
usually ran up as much as $50,000–75,000 in outstanding loans,
using five men to "collect" from debt-ridden families when
their payments fell due. Fortunately most people in Henry
Hawkins' position never know what it is like to deal with these
merchants of despair. While Henry is busy learning about
municipal bonds, the poor are learning what it is like to survive
"on the street," often at a high cost.

The major sources of credit and their shares of the market
appear in Figure 13. Notice that the lion's share of business is
done by commercial banks. Over 260 million bank credit cards,
such as Master Charge and BankAmericard, and "prestige"
cards such as Diner's Club and American Express, capture a
bare 5 percent of the $120 billion charged in 1970. In fact, the
major issuers of write-your-own ticket credit are the big retail
merchants, department stores, and mercantile chains that maintain their own operations. These giants, together with the
airline and oil companies, granted by far the greatest portion
of the total credit available to consumers.[14] Note too that automobile credit forms a large share of the total consumer credit
shown in Figure 13. This discrepancy is due largely to the fact

[12] *Black, p. 159.*
[13] *David Caplovitz,* The Poor Pay More *(New York: The Free Press,
1967).*
[14] *Griffin, p. 43.*

Figure 13

SOURCES OF CONSUMER CREDIT

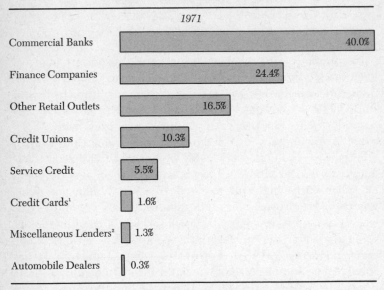

1971

Commercial Banks	40.0%
Finance Companies	24.4%
Other Retail Outlets	16.5%
Credit Unions	10.3%
Service Credit	5.5%
Credit Cards¹	1.6%
Miscellaneous Lenders²	1.3%
Automobile Dealers	0.3%

¹Not including bank credit card accounts.
²Including savings and loan associations and mutual savings banks.

Source: Board of Governors, *Federal Reserve Bulletin*, 58, 5, Washington, D.C. (May 1972), A56–A57.

that most automobile credit is held by finance companies, banks, and credit unions.

A CREDITABLE PERFORMANCE

A consumer's credit rating gives him access to a vast network of credit institutions that bestow their riches on the fortunate few. Thus it is useful to consider the mechanism by which a credit seeker is rated. At the heart of the process lies a set of criteria that define a "good" credit applicant. These are based both on studies of what characteristics affect a person's ability to pay off a loan and/or on the cumulative wisdom of the employees of the credit bureau. Illustrative of these characteristics are such items as a person's occupation, length of time at work, residence, marital status, and financial condition. Each characteristic is assigned a number of points, and the number of points a person receives determines his or her credit worthiness. By establishing a numerical threshold beyond which credit will automatically be granted, these modern day guardians of the golden fleece claim to have introduced a measure of objectivity into an erstwhile subjective process.

To underscore the effects of these so-called objective criteria, we shall consider the rating scheme used by a large midwestern credit bureau. Table 13 shows the points assigned to each of several attributes of an individual. Appropriate points are determined for each rating category and then added to derive a total score. This score serves to summarize a person's credit worthiness for those seeking information about a client's credit rating. Applicants who score 30 or more are considered good credit risks; those with ratings below 13 are automatically denied credit; and those in between are subject to further review.

Henry Mews is a business executive, has held his present job for seven years, owns a home in which he has lived for six years, is married, earns over $200 a week, has both a checking and a savings account, and holds two gasoline credit cards. On the credit scale Mews receives 40 points—10 points above the score required for automatic credit acceptance. Herbert Munstler is not as fortunate. His credit rating, based on the criteria just listed, is 28. This means that his case is subject to further review, and his credit rating will depend on the good graces of the local credit bureau. Harry Albright is a recent college graduate temporarily working as a door-to-door salesman in order to earn enough money to return to school. On the job less than one year, renting a room, single, earning $100 a week, and with only a savings account, Harry is likely to be denied access to less costly forms of credit. He is a potential victim for a small finance company or a loan shark.

While the criteria listed earlier do not in and of themselves favor a particular group, it is hardly likely that they penalize the wealthy. In the worst of straits a rich man who does not own his own home, is divorced, earns over $200 a week, has

Table 13

CRITERIA USED TO RATE A CREDIT APPLICANT

1. Occupation	Points	2. Job Tenure	Points	6. Weekly Earnings	Points
Business executives	7	Present job less		Over $200	5
Doctors & dentists	7	than 2 years;		$101 to $200	4
College professors	7	previous job less		$91 to $100	3
Scientists	6	than 10 years	1	$76 to $90	2
Office clerical help	6	Present job 2 to		$61 to $75	1
Farmers	6	5 years; previous		$60 or less	0
Nurses	5	job 10 years or			
Skilled factory		more	3	7. Bank Accounts	
workers	5	Present job 7 years		Both checking &	
Editors	5	or more; previous		savings	6
Plumbers	4	job less than		Savings only	3
Lawyers & judges	4	10 years	5	Checking only	2
Soldiers & sailors	4				
Freelance writers	3	3. Residence		8. Credit References	
Janitors	3	Own home	5	2 gasoline credit	
Barbers	3	Renting house or		cards	4
Longshoremen	2	apartment	3	2 department store	
Bartenders	2	Living with parents		cards	4
Garage workers	2	or relatives	3	1 gasoline card	2
Musicians	1	Renting room or		1 department store	
Domestic servants	1	trailer	0	card	2
Painters	1			1 finance company	−2
Door-to-door		4. Time at Present		1 credit jewelry	
salesmen	0	Residence		store*	−2
Farm laborers	0	Over 5 years	3	2 finance	
Cab drivers	0	2 to 5 years	2	companies	−4
		Less than 2 years	1	2 credit jewelry	
				stores*	−4
		5. Marital Status			
		Married	5		
		Widowed	5		
		Single woman	4		
		Single man	3		
		Divorced woman	2		
		Separated	0		
		Divorced man	0		

*Indicates number of pieces of jewelry bought on credit.

Source: Al Griffin, The Credit Jungle (Chicago: Henry Regnery Co., 1971), pp. 158–160.

both a checking and a savings account, and has two gasoline or department store credit cards receives a meager 21 points. In the credit review that follows, however, he will probably be granted an acceptable credit rating. On the other hand, people with low incomes and no prior credit history are likely to be unacceptable as credit risks. Woe to the young bartender, domestic worker, cab driver, or farm laborer who needs an extra shot of credit to keep his family going. And the divorced woman struggling to make ends meet at $80 a week may well feel that the system is against her. It certainly is!

THE DISPARITY OF INTEREST RATES

Although most economics textbooks talk of *the* interest rate as if there were a single rate, the preceding discussion suggests the presence of a number of borrowing rates, with access to the lowest rate depending on a satisfactory credit rating. Does the existence of several rates reflect a conscious attempt by society to make life easy for the wealthy and difficult for the poor, or is it a result of inexorable forces at work in the market-place? The existence of several borrowing rates can be explained by differences in the conditions under which consumer funds are demanded by and supplied to borrowers. To understand these conditions let us consider the lending hierarchy.

Commercial banks are the primary beneficiaries of expansionary Federal Reserve (Fed) monetary policies. When the Fed wishes to speed up the growth of the economy, it increases the reserves of commercial banks. A portion of these reserves is then used to make commercial and installment loans to eligible borrowers. If funds are relatively plentiful, and assuming that customers with good credit ratings have access to a number of banks, competition will ensure that the borrowing rate charged these customers is low. Moreover, since very few highly rated customers default on their loans and most pay off their loans promptly when due, commercial banks can charge a low fee for administering a loan.

When the Fed cuts back on bank reserves, commercial banks find it necessary to restrict credit. This may be done either by raising the interest rate at which loans are granted (thus decreasing the number of people wishing to borrow if other things remain the same) or by restricting lending to their largest and most valued customers. Although considerable research has been done on the responsiveness of banks to changes in the money supply, remarkably little information exists on the distribution of loans by income class during hard times. Nonetheless, there is *a priori* evidence to indicate that loans are granted primarily to the well-to-do. During times

when money is tight, low- and middle-income housing starts
tend to decrease substantially, perhaps reflecting the difficulty
of obtaining mortgages. And small businessmen (especially
those with limited credit histories) find it difficult to borrow,
particularly when their companies cannot tap the commercial
paper or bond markets. Although some large companies find
that limited credit is available during a money crunch, the
"blue chips" are usually the last to feel the pinch.

Lending institutions other than banks must normally pay
more to acquire the funds they lend to others. These institutions may borrow directly from commercial banks, but this
usually entails a price above the prime rate. Alternatively, they
may acquire funds from other sources such as insurance companies and the bond and stock markets. However, such lenders
usually require a higher borrowing rate to compensate for the
greater risk they face in dealing with nonbank customers.

Large borrowers like Beneficial Corp., Household Finance,
and GMAC receive loan funds from a variety of sources. In
1971, for example, GMAC borrowed nearly $7.7 billion in the
United States. Of the $4.1 billion payable in one year, $3.9
billion was financed by commercial paper and only $4 million
by bank borrowings. GMAC's lenders required, and received,
a borrowing rate somewhat higher than the prime rate charged
by commercial banks.[15] Correspondingly, the rate GMAC
charged most of its borrowers was higher than that charged
by banks.

The highest borrowing costs are incurred by small finance
companies and loan sharks. Since loans granted by these
lenders are extremely risky, capital suppliers demand a very
high return on their investments. In one case a loan shark's
"downtown" connection charged a flat *1 percent per week*.
Thus for $10,000 the loan shark paid $100 weekly. In addition
to high capital costs, loan sharks also face high default rates
and substantial collection costs. Although the days of the
omnipotent Al Capone appear to be over, many loan sharks
continue to hire "toughs" to make sure that loans are paid on
time. The cost of these "collectors," as well as a generous pay-

[15] GMAC Annual Report, 1971.

ment for the loan shark's time, are charged to borrowers through a high interest rate. The implications of this type of financing are nicely summed up by James Baldwin's remark that "anyone who has ever struggled with poverty knows how extremely expensive it is to be poor."

Thus far we have discussed only the supply side of the market for loanable funds, but demand factors are also relevant. Wealthy customers may have recourse to several sources of loans. In time of need they can borrow from friends, make loans against their insurance policies, or even reduce their holdings of stocks and bonds. If funds are unavailable they may postpone purchasing nonessential durable goods until the money market loosens. As a result the demand for funds by the rich is likely to be responsive to changes in the interest rate. This is not the case for the poor. Unable to receive funds from several sources, they are usually at the mercy of one or two small-loan companies or of the local loan shark. And many times the financial needs of the poor are urgent and cannot be met by putting off nonessential expenditures for "better" times. The demand for funds by poor families is likely to be unresponsive to the borrowing rate. Thus while the poor are subject to the discipline of the marketplace, the rich have other options.

LIMITS TO COMPETITION

Although interest rates are set in the marketplace, the market for funds is not a perfectly competitive one. Under present federal regulations, for example, banks and other interest-paying institutions cannot pay small depositors as much as larger ones. In 1935, the Federal Reserve's Regulation Q was enacted in order to prevent unbridled competition. Under this measure commercial banks, and more recently, savings and loan associations and mutual savings banks are limited in the amounts they can pay depositors. Since 1965, when the combination of a booming economy and deficit spending sent prices and interest rates soaring, Regulation Q has depressed the yields of savings accounts relative to other assets. In mid-1965, for example, a short-term business loan might have earned about 5 percent. By 1969, a similar loan earned 9 percent. During the same period Treasury bill rates rose from 4 percent to a little over 9 percent; equally large increases occurred in the interest on commercial paper and other debt instruments. Nonetheless, the rates on ordinary savings accounts issued at commercial banks remained constant until January 1970, when they rose slightly to 4.5 percent.[16]

What makes the differential between the various types of financial instruments and savings deposits especially significant is that the latter assets are held primarily by people with low incomes. According to the *Federal Reserve Survey*, for example, almost 29 percent of all savings deposits are held by people with incomes of less than $5,000, while 60 percent belong to people with incomes under $10,000.[17] Furthermore, over 60 percent of the latter group hold no other financial assets.[18] By comparison, only 7 percent of the knights and 4 percent of those with incomes between $50,000 and $100,000 hold no other financial assets.[19] The greater a consumer unit's income, the greater the options available to him. Thus the effect of using Regulation Q to hold down interest rates is to discriminate against people with low incomes.

Public financial organizations—primarily the Treasury, Securities and Exchange Commission, and Federal Reserve—play an important role in maintaining the war for wealth. In a highly imaginative paper James Gatti and Steven Weiss point out several weapons used in fighting the war. These include policies designed to eliminate small-denomination Treasury bills, to encourage high brokerage rates on small investments, to appeal to patriotism as a means of selling low-interest U.S. savings bonds to unsophisticated small investors, and to restrict "mini-bonds" (which, when issued in small denominations, are an excellent substitute for time deposits from the consumer's point of view).[20]

---

[16] *James Gatti and Steven Weiss, "Big Money and Small Potatoes," unpublished paper, p. 5.*
[17] *Dorothy Projector and Gertrude Weiss,* Survey of Financial Characteristics of Consumers, *Federal Reserve Technical Papers, August 1966, pp. 126, 132. Hereafter referred to as* Federal Reserve Survey.
[18] Federal Reserve Survey, *p. 138.*
[19] Federal Reserve Survey, *p. 138.*
[20] *Gatti and Weiss, p. 14.*

Through policies like these the government ensures that people who have money to begin with can earn more on their investments than those who do not. To see how these policies affect wealthy investors, we shall consider the life cycle.

OLDER AND WISER

Researchers exploring consumption and spending patterns have found that the percentage of a family's income used for consumption depends on the family's position in the life cycle. Families with a household head under the age of 35 usually have a high ratio of consumption to income, using most of their funds to establish a household and to raise children. In fact, many young families, particularly those with low incomes, go into debt to meet their needs. As these families get older their savings rise and they are able to pay off old debts and accumulate assets. At some point family income reaches a peak and stabilizes. Then, as the household head approaches and reaches retirement age, a new pattern sets in. Savings begin to fall and the assets accumulated over the course of a lifetime are used to provide retirement income.

Does the life cycle affect the borrowing decisions made by the wealthy? If it did we would expect to find a family accumulating debt in the earlier and later years (if at all), while reducing its debt in the intermediate period when family income is high. Unfortunately, limited data are available for studying this question. Those shown in Figure 14 come from the 1962 *Federal Reserve Survey*. Since this study provides only the *interval* within which a consumer unit's debt falls, exact figures for the amount of debt held by a family at a particular income level cannot be shown.[21] Similarly, since consumer unit income data are also reported by interval rather than exact amount, our discussion is confined to an analysis of the debt holdings of the representative (median) rather than the average (mean) consumer unit.

Debt holdings by the age and income of consumer units can

[21] *Note that the data presented here are for consumer units and not for families. Since consumer units include both families and single individuals, they may provide somewhat different results than data for families alone. Such differences are likely to be quite small.*

Figure 14

DEBT HOLDINGS BY FAMILY AGE AND INCOME

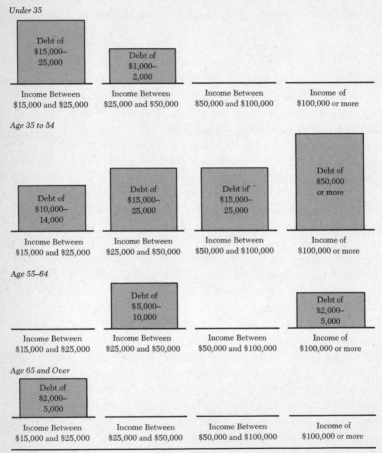

Source: Dorothy Projector and Gertrude Weiss, *Survey of Financial Characteristics of Consumers,* Federal Reserve Technical Papers, August 1966, p. 106.

be used to examine the effects of the life cycle by income group. In general, the age-debt pattern observed in the $10,000–15,000 income group follows the pattern described earlier. A representative consumer unit head with an annual income of $15,000–25,000 accumulates debt at a young age, pays off a portion of that debt between the ages of 35 and 54, and has no debt between the ages of 55 and 64. After retirement some new debt is created. This pattern does not hold for the representative consumer unit head with an income of over $25,000. In consumer units with heads below the age of 35, debt holdings are inversely related to income. But the representative consumer unit with a head between the ages of 35 and 54 holds *more* debt as its income *rises*.

Why do consumer units headed by people between the ages of 35 and 54 with incomes above $25,000 accumulate more debt than others? And why does the amount of debt held increase with income? The answer seems to rest with the differences in the borrowing motives of the various income groups. Low-income units borrow primarily to finance the purchase of a home or of durable consumer goods. High-income units borrow for these reasons too but also use borrowed funds to take advantage of the myriad of investment opportunities available to them.

When the debt held by the representative unit at each income level above $25,000 is broken down into three components—personal, home, and investment—this point is dramatically borne out. Personal debt holdings, including such items as automobile, appliance, and cash loans, appear to be unrelated to income. Housing debt rises with income at an increasing rate and then levels off around the $50,000 income level (see Chapter 1). Interestingly, however, investment debt, represented by such items as stocks, bonds, and real estate, *rises* directly with income. Moreover, this type of debt is heavily concentrated in units headed by people between the ages of 35 and 54. Thus the increase in debt as income rises appears to be due primarily to the increase in the demand for investment assets.

It is not surprising to find an increase in debt among units in the 35–54 group once it is recognized that this is the age at which people try to increase their wealth through investment. In fact, when the *net* wealth of such units is examined, the data show that they are not debtors. In 1962 the representative consumer unit with an income between $15,000 and $24,000 had a net worth between $25,000 and $50,000. With an income between $25,000 and $50,000, the representative unit had a net worth between $100,000 and $200,000, and an income between

$50,000 and $100,000 was related to a net worth of $200,000
to $500,000. Units with incomes of $100,000 or more had a
median net worth between $500,000 and $1 million.[22] This
evidence, after adjustment for the investment motive, appears
to be consistent with the life cycle pattern.

INVESTMENT OPPORTUNITIES AND THE WEALTHY

Even if the policies governing the nation's financial institutions
did not favor the rich, the odds would still be in their favor.
Those in the knight and warlord income groups have access to
more information about existing investment opportunities than
others and may also be privy to new investment ventures. By
virtue of their wealth these investors can expend the large
sums required to buy shares in oil exploration funds, real-
estate trusts, and housing syndicates. And the tax laws both
increase the returns and lower the costs that the rich incur in
realizing their investments.

Investment in stocks, bonds, real estate, and small businesses
is often a long and costly affair. In the up-and-down markets
of the late sixties and early seventies, few low-income investors
made money. As Fred C. Kelly, an expert on the stock market,
wrote in 1930, "The crowd always loses because the crowd is
always wrong. It is wrong because it behaves normally."
Simply investigating a company's balance sheets or monthly
reports does not provide an investor with the assurance of a
sure-fire gain. Gerald Loeb put the matter well: "There is no
such thing as a final answer to security values. A dozen experts
will arrive at 12 different conclusions. It often happens that a
few moments later each would alter his verdict if given a
chance to reconsider because of a changed condition."[23]

Even those able to pay the price of a leading advisory
service can be disappointed, as thousands of investors learned
in 1968–1970. It takes a pro to make money on Wall Street,
and even pros can be wrong. Said John Maynard Keynes of the
stock market, ". . . it is, so to speak a game of Snap, of Old
Maid, of Musical Chairs—a pastime in which he is victor who

[22] Federal Reserve Survey, pp. 98–99.
[23] Adam Smith, The Money Game (New York: Dell Publishing Co.,
Inc., 1969), p. 43.

says *Snap* neither too soon nor too late, who passes the Old Maid to his neighbor before the game is over, who secures a chair for himself before the music stops."[24] Nonetheless, the investor willing to pay the price of an adviser may be better off than a lone individual playing a hunch.

Investment possibilities in real estate and housing also favor people with high incomes. The icing on the investor's cake is the special tax advantage he gains through real-estate invest- ment. Accelerated depreciation and capital gains treatment of property held several years raise the rates of return on real estate to 15 percent, 20 percent, or even more. And in cases in which depreciation is a large part of the investment cost, the tax laws are particularly kind to investors. Unfortunately, few low-income investors can benefit from these provisions, even if they are aware of the existence of good tax shelters. Their tax brackets are simply too low to allow the huge tax savings claimed by the wealthy.

Many of the investment opportunities that provide a high return on investment can be obtained only by the wealthy. Participation in an oil exploration venture usually requires a minimum investment of $25,000 to $50,000. And syndicates that sell shares in shopping centers, hotels, apartment complexes, and other real-estate ventures often require investors to give up $100,000 or more. Especially in cases involving high closing costs and legal fees, the small investor simply cannot afford the costs of entry.

In recent years Wall Street has tapped the funds of small investors through real-estate investment trusts (REITs). Such trusts enable the small investor to purchase real estate by pooling his resources with others. Unfortunately the perfor- mance of these funds has been spotty; while they often yield returns of 9–10 percent, this is about half the potential return available to the person who invests directly in a sound real- estate deal. Moreover, many small investors have never heard of REITs.

Closely related to the size of an investor's holdings is the issue of risk. By spreading out funds over a variety of situa- tions, the clever investor can bring the probability of loss to

[24] *Smith, p. 186.*

an acceptable level while at the same time increasing his average return. Of course, the small investor may obtain the same end by buying shares of a mutual fund. But mutual funds charge management fees, and some add a "loading charge" that reduces the return. In almost all areas of investment, then, the odds are heavily in favor of the wealthy.

TAXES AND INTEREST

Through favorable treatment of interest payments, the tax laws reduce the cost to the wealthy who borrow money. This is a puzzling direction for public policy, since it reinforces the advantages already bestowed by the marketplace. The tax laws governing borrowing provide yet another example of the internalization policies promulgated by the government—policies difficult to justify except by the type of logic described throughout this book.

At issue here is the provision of the tax law that permits a taxpayer to deduct interest payments made during the year from his tax return. At first glance this would seem to benefit low-income families paying exorbitant interest rates. But the reality differs from the illusion. First, although the poor may pay interest that represents a large share of their incomes, the absolute amount they borrow is less than that borrowed by the well-to-do. In the *1970 Survey of Consumer Finance,* for example, over 50 percent of the in-debt families reporting incomes below $3,000 had debts ranging between $1 and $199. Among families with incomes of $15,000 or more, less than 10 percent of families had debts this low, while over 59 percent had debts of $2,000 or more.[25]

Moreover, the simple mathematics of wealth apply to the interest deduction. For example, a taxpayer in the 70 percent tax bracket who takes out a loan at a 9 percent borrowing rate can deduct 6.3 cents out of every dollar (70 percent of the initial 9 percent rate) on his tax return. As a result his posttax borrowing rate is only 2.7 percent. A pretax 9 percent borrowing rate works out to a posttax rate of 4.5 percent for the

[23] 1970 Survey of Consumer Finance, *p. 23.*

taxpayer in the 50 percent tax bracket, 6.3 percent for the one in the 30 percent bracket, and 8.1 percent for the one in the 10 percent bracket.

Because the tax laws are set up so that the value of the interest deduction rises with income, the wealthy pay less interest (after taxes) than the poor. The tax statistics clearly reveal the beneficiaries of the system. According to recent estimates, about 70 percent of the over $5 billion in mortgage interest deductions for owner-occupied homes are claimed by taxpayers with $10,000 or more.[26]

Moreover, some of the wealthiest people in the country pay little or no tax as a result of the interest deduction. In 1970 Representative Gibbons made the following remarks to the House Committee on Banking and Currency:

> I think all of you will remember last year we were talking about those 154 taxpayers who had incomes of more than $200,000 in 1967 and paid no income tax; and you perhaps wondered how they got out of all taxes . . . the greatest reason for their not paying income tax was the high interest deduction . . . in fact, 74 of those 154 taxpayers were able to reduce their tax to zero because they made maximum use of being able to write off interest cost. Again in 1968, various individual taxpayers were collectively able to deduct $18.5 billion in interest . . . and in 1966, the last year we have figures for, corporations deducted $31.3 billion in interest from their taxes.[27]

When the tax provisions dealing with the deduction of interest are combined with the provisions affecting the return on a taxpayer's investment, such as capital gains, they provide a hefty incentive for the wealthy to invest borrowed funds. By obtaining funds at low interest rates and taking advantage of the tax laws to boost their yearly returns, the wealthy can increase their incomes. The thrust of government policy favors the wealthy, who, as usual, are not slow to recognize where their advantage lies.

[26] *U.S. Congress, Joint Economic Committee, "The Economics of Federal Subsidy Programs" (January 1972), p. 45.*

[27] *House Committee on Banking and Currency, "A Call for a Rollback of High Interest Rates" (March 24, 1970), pp. 11–12.*

9
THE EDUCATIONAL SORT

The social class inequalities in our school system and the role they play in the reproduction of the social division of labor are too evident to be denied. Defenders of the educational system are forced back on the assertion that things are getting better; the inequalities of the past have been mitigated. . . . Yet new inequalities have apparently developed to take their place, for the available historical evidence lends little support to the idea that our schools are on the road to equality of educational opportunity.

—SAMUEL BOWLES

Education has provided hope to egalitarians for hundreds of years. While the war for wealth may be fought elsewhere, the little red schoolhouse is a place where anyone may go, irrespective of his family's income, in order to seek an improved position in life. Mass education provides a means by which the intergenerational inequities of the past can be redressed and each generation gets a fresh start. Such is the myth that many Americans believe and that has led to the creation of one of the largest educational establishments the world has ever known.

Reality presents a different story, however. From the time a child is conceived by wealthy parents to the moment he or she enters the labor force, that individual never outgrows the advantages of wealth. It takes money to enable a child's potential intelligence to be realized. And it takes a fairly decent income to provide the type of environment that helps a child register a high score on the measured "intelligence" tests. Money can be used to purchase a home in a community with a "good" school system or to send a child to a private school. It can also buy an education at the "right" university. From the cradle to the job market, the policies of the educational establishment tend to lock a student into place, reinforcing the differences created by the war for wealth.

THE ABCs OF INTELLIGENCE

In order to understand how the schools facilitate the war for wealth, it will be useful to distinguish between three types of intelligence: Intelligence A involves an individual's potential at the moment of conception; Intelligence B, his or her potential at birth; and Intelligence C, realized intelligence after birth. Although a person's environment cannot affect Intelligence A, it does affect B and C. Intelligence A is created when the genes of two parents join to determine their child's potential; it places an outer limit on the amount of intelligence an individual can acquire in a lifetime. Several things can happen before birth, however, and these help to determine Intelligence B. Malnutrition, sickness, and exposure to dangerous diseases may lower or even destroy the potential for intelligence. The conditions under which an infant is delivered also affect its Intelligence B. If complications develop while the child is being born, for example, it may enter the world with its ability to learn greatly impaired.

The environment in which a fetus develops and is delivered depends to some extent on the income of its parents. Thus even if Intelligence A is distributed randomly among members of the population, infants from wealthy homes are more likely to realize their Intelligence A potential than those conceived in families with lower incomes.

After birth, environmental influences affect the infant directly. Intelligence B affects the way a baby responds to its environment. But the environment in which the child grows up also influences the ideas he is exposed to and the frequency of contact with new learning experiences. Thus Intelligence C

reflects the combined effects of heredity and environment. It is
this form of "natural" intelligence that IQ and other aptitude
tests attempt to capture.

Measures of IQ are usually highly correlated with measures
of socioeconomic status. This would be true even if an ideal
measure of IQ could be found. Where the measure is less than
ideal, the biases of those preparing the test of intelligence
make these measures even more strongly related to family
background. As a result IQ and other aptitude scores are
dubious measures of natural intelligence at best.

THE SELECTION AND SORTING PROCESS

Among the very rich the young are sent off to learn at top-
flight private institutions. Most children in estate class, knight,
and warlord families are not as fortunate. For these children
the public schools must suffice. Over time, however, a system
has evolved that tends to segregate those from higher-income
homes, usually permitting them to receive a more intensive
form of instruction. This system serves to restrict upward
mobility and to increase the opportunities available to those
from affluent homes.

The founders of the public-school system tried to ensure
that every child would receive an education irrespective of his
family's income or social status. But their original intent was
quickly subverted. As the system evolved, an open-door policy
at the neighborhood school constituted *prima facie* evidence
that everyone had an equal education. The existence of different educational curricula and other schemes for separating
one group from another within a school was largely ignored.
Yet as William Faulkner puts it, "There is no such thing as
equality *per se*, but only equality to: equal right and opportunity to make the best of one's life within one's capacity and
capability, without fear of injustice or oppression or violence."[1]
In theory, all students of public-school age have an equal right

---

[1] *William Faulkner, "On Fear: Deep South in Labor: Mississippi," in
James B. Meriweather (ed.),* Essays; Public Speeches and Public Letters
by William Faulkner *(New York: Random House, Inc., 1965), p. 105.*

and opportunity to receive a good education. In practice, this right is rarely recognized. This is a natural concomitant of the war for wealth.

The public schools play an important role in shaping the minds of future generations. They develop the characteristics of punctuality, obedience, and discipline in children from lower- and middle-class homes. And they breed respect for educated people. Moreover, they present information that their students will carry with them throughout life. What better way to ensure the success of the war for wealth than to encourage policies favorable to the preservation of the status quo? And what better method to ensure the rigidity of the existing income distribution than to channel students into different schooling choices based on their measured IQ's?[2] Such tests, at first glance, are objective, unbiased, and value-free. By assigning "bright" students to a college curriculum and "slower" ones to a vocational program, the schools claim to help everyone find his own level.

It took many years before social reformers began to realize that students were being passed through a golden screen. In the interim the warriors for wealth watched from the sidelines, calm in their belief that the jobs held by the next generation would be similar to those held by the last, assured of a stable and well-trained labor force and an electorate remarkably unaware of the war for wealth.

THE GOLDEN SCREEN

At first most educators expressed satisfaction with the use of IQ measures as a basis for sorting students. Why not provide the best opportunities to the brightest students? Wouldn't the world be a better place if the schools created a favored class made up of the "able" rather than the wealthy? Didn't the

---

[2] *For an opposite viewpoint to the one presented here, see Christopher Jencks,* Inequality: A Reassessment of the Effect of Family and Schooling in America *(New York: Basic Books, Inc., 1972). According to Jencks, ". . . if an economic elite wanted to pass along its privileges to its children, establishing a system in which privilege depended on test scores would not be a wise strategy" (p. 81). But the methodology used by Jencks to arrive at this conclusion has been subject to considerable criticism.*

grocer's daughter have as much chance to succeed as the banker's daughter? It sounded very reasonable, but there was an important catch: Measured IQ and family background are correlated. Thus a process that channels students on the basis of IQ may also separate the rich and the poor.

The importance of this point should not be minimized. In an excellent study of a large city in the Midwest, for example, Patricia Sexton collected IQ, achievement, and family income data from over 300 schools. She found three very interesting things: (1) Students whose parents have an average income above $7,000 a year achieve scores above the average grade level. Likewise those whose parents' incomes average below $7,000 achieve scores below the average grade level. (2) Student achievement and IQ scores tend to rise in schools with high average family incomes, and for the IQ scores the rise is quite significant. (3) Students in the highest income group have average achievement scores almost *two full years* above those in the lowest income group by the time they reach the eighth grade. These results are shown in Table 14.

As this table suggests, sorting students by IQ or achievement results in a separation of the different socioeconomic groups. If one group is labeled "bright" and another "dull," this procedure may result in a stigma that low-income students carry with them for the rest of their lives. Sexton states the matter well:

> . . . it seems that one very destructive function of the IQ
> score is that it serves as a kind of cement which fixes
> students into the social classes of their birth. IQ is the
> supreme and unchallengeable justification for the social class
> system. . . . Just as the right to rule was given to kings by
> God, so is the right to rule given to the upper classes by
> "nature" and by virtue of what they presume to be their
> superior IQ's.[3]

IQ tests are strongly biased in favor of middle-class values. Such tests pose questions frequently encountered in urban

[3] *Patricia Sexton,* Education and Income *(New York: The Viking Press, Inc., 1961), p. 51.*

Table 14

ACHIEVEMENT, IQ, AND FAMILY INCOME IN BIG CITY

Family Income	Grade Level Achievement on Iowa Achievement Test*	IQ Score**
Fourth Grade		
$3,000–5,000	3.48	2.79
$5,000–7,000	3.73	3.31
$7,000–9,000	4.42	4.55
$9,000–12,000	4.84	5.09
Difference between highest and lowest groups	1.36	2.30
Sixth Grade		
$3,000–5,000	5.23	
$5,000–7,000	5.61	
$7,000–9,000	6.47	
$9,000–12,000	7.05	
Difference between highest and lowest groups	1.82	
Eighth Grade		
$3,000–5,000	6.77	
$5,000–7,000	7.38	
$7,000–9,000	8.22	
$9,000–12,000	8.67	
Difference between highest and lowest groups	1.90	

* The Iowa Achievement Test is nationally standardized in terms of grade equivalents. The above scores are the sum of scores in language skills, word skills, arithmetic skills, reading, and vocabulary.

** The IQ scores shown above refer to the combined scores of children in the first and fourth grades.

Source: Patricia Sexton, *Education and Income* (New York: The Viking Press, Inc., 1961), pp. 28, 39.

middle-class environments. Naturally, middle- and upper-income students find these easier to answer. Moreover, differences in IQ scores may be due to the greater vocabularies of children from higher-income homes. This makes IQ a poor proxy for natural ability. Furthermore, students from such homes frequently perform better on IQ tests because they are more highly motivated and more knowledgeable and have a more sophisticated attitude toward tests. Since researchers have been unable to isolate economic factors in measuring IQ, they have used care in interpreting IQ scores as a measure of intelligence.[4]

Nonetheless, most schools continue to use IQ as a proxy for natural intelligence. Many devote their best resources to the "brightest" students. Tracking systems and similar schemes ensure that students from low-income homes progress through the school system at a slower rate than their peers. The tracking system separates children into learning programs such as "college preparatory," "general," and "vocational"; a different set of courses is then designed to meet the best interests of the students in each track. Such a system favors students who manage to enter a higher track at an earlier age, usually those from affluent families. Participants in the college program are often taught by the best teachers, read the most up-to-date textbooks, and receive the most advanced teaching techniques. By contrast, those in the lowest tracks are "warehoused" until they leave to take their place on an assembly line or in some unskilled job.

Of course, a few gifted students from low-income homes manage to pass through the golden screen, and some even manage to rise to a position of prominence in society. The existence of a limited amount of upward mobility lends legitimacy to the myth that the public schools provide an equal opportunity to all. And it disguises the stratification that takes place within the educational system. Students with low IQ scores who become increasingly aware of their status in the system simply give up. As the statistics in Table 15 suggest, big-city schools fail to capture the interest of students from low-income homes. Statistically speaking, these students are the casualties of existing policies.

---

[4] *It should be recalled, however, that a student's genes as well as his family's economic status will affect his performance on a measured IQ test.*

Table 15

ATTENDANCE, DROPOUTS, AND FAMILY
INCOME IN BIG-CITY SCHOOLS

Income Group	Attendance During a Typical Week (Percent)	Dropouts (Percent)
$5,000–6,000	90.6	19.2
6,000–7,000	92.7	15.8
7,000–8,000	94.3	7.9
8,000–9,000	94.8	7.2
9,000 or more	94.9	3.6

Source: Patricia Sexton, *Education and Income* (New York: The Viking Press, Inc., 1961), pp. 157, 202.

As W. Lloyd Warner, Robert Havighurst, and Martin Loeb see the school system in operation, "One large group of students is almost immediately brushed off into a bin labelled 'non-readers,' 'first-grade repeaters,' or 'opportunity class,' where they stay for eight to ten years and are then released through a chute to the outside world to become 'hewers of wood and drawers of water.' "[5] And thanks to the school system, wood hewing is an occupation that may be passed down from father to son.

The very rich send their children to "preparatory" schools, which prepare them for entry to the nation's top colleges and universities. These schools screen out "unsuitable" students and help instill a set of values appropriate to future warriors for wealth. While some schools teach discipline, most are far more concerned with graduating students wise in the ways of the world and equipped with the basic academic skills. The "warehousing" policies of the public schools are foreign to this group and touch on their lives only insofar as they affect the availability of a trained labor force and the maintenance of a stable political order.

Nonetheless, many children from knight and warlord homes

[5] W. Lloyd Warner, Robert Havighurst, and Martin Loeb, Who Shall Be Educated? (New York: Harper & Row, Publishers, Inc., 1944).

receive their education in the public schools. It is these children who benefit directly from the present policies of the school authorities. Under the existing system many affluent families can buy a high-priced education for their children at a cost to the less intelligent (affluent) children in the school. The golden screen provides a convenient mechanism by which taxes supporting the public schools may be used to provide a high-cost education to students from wealthy homes. And when too many "bright" low-income children enter the school system, wealthy families can always move to another community that offers a more attractive school system and, sometimes, a lower school tax. We shall call this migration to ghettolike enclaves of wealth "the localization of wealth."

THE LOCALIZATION OF WEALTH

Local control of the schools provides an important linchpin in the battle for control of schools by the affluent. Through local control those living in wealthy communities can ensure that their children receive the best resources available. For while the experts may differ on whether the amounts spent on education actually affect what students learn, many parents continue to seek out expensive-looking schools with high-paid teachers. Indeed, for many families the day-to-day benefits of attending a modern school with children from "good" homes are sufficiently important so that they will move to a new location in order to send their children to a "good" school.

Of course, one rarely finds the principle of local control argued on the basis of its advantages to the wealthy. Instead its advocates argue that low-level decision making preserves the freedom and independence of the populace. They also see local interest and participation in community affairs as important concomitants of low-level control. Analyzing the efficiency of local control, Charles Tiebout states:

> Instead of taking the people as given and trying to fit the nonnational public goods pattern to them, offer a varied pattern of public goods and make it possible for the people to move to suit their tastes. People who want good schools will then be able to move to communities where good

schools are provided. To the extent that communities offer
a varied pattern of public goods, each resident can, con-
ceptually, choose the pattern which best satisfies his
preference.[6]

Tiebout's analysis assumes, of course, that families have the
financial resources to indulge their tastes.

Several other arguments have been used to buttress the case
for local control. Since the educational needs of children differ
from one school district to another, the people who live in an
area are better able to evaluate what must be spent in their
own district. Moreover, in locally managed districts the boun-
ties of good management remain close to home. These may be
reflected either in lower tax rates or in greater resource use
per pupil. Furthermore, a plurality of thoughtful and independent decision makers may stimulate interdistrict competition. Since school districts (as opposed to individual schools)
have greater freedom to utilize any teaching methods they
wish, competition may lead to the discovery and implementation of new teaching techniques.

Whatever other advantages it may possess, local control is
uniquely suited to the needs of wealthy families. Recognizing
this, Tiebout writes:

> At the real world level, the existence of unequal income
> has led to the "tax colony." That is, people with high incomes
> band together in communities which keep low income
> residents out. . . . When you seek good schools for your
> children, you often find the rents and housing prices are
> high. This is not to suggest any single direct causality . . .
> it is simply a suggestion as to how . . . the rich avoid paying
> taxes for the poor.[7]

High-priced neighborhoods usually have a large wealth
base. Therefore they can levy a lower tax rate to raise money
for the schools than poorer neighborhoods can.[8] This makes it

---

[6] *Charles Tiebout, "An Economic Theory of Fiscal Decentralization,"
in James Buchanan (ed.), Public Finances: Needs, Sources, and Utiliza-
tion (Princeton, N.J.: Princeton University Press, 1961), pp. 92–93.*

[7] *Tiebout, p. 94.*

[8] *This is not true of all low-income districts, however. Some have a
large wealth base because of the presence of local industry.*

cheaper for a wealthy person to own a $50,000 home in a wealthy district than in a poor one. Differences in district wealth can be enormous! For example, a 1966–1967 study of high school districts in Cook County, Ill., found that the wealth of these districts ranged from $31,000 to $108,200 per pupil— thus the wealthiest district had a base three-and-one-half times that of the poorest.[9] By living in high-priced neighborhoods, the wealthy can provide high-quality schooling for their children at a relatively low cost to themselves.

Because wealth (as measured by district assessed property valuation) is unequally distributed among school districts, people with limited incomes living in "poor" school districts find it difficult to provide adequate schooling for their young. Foundation plans created by the states are designed to provide an equalizing state contribution to each district. Nonetheless, most of these plans fail to ease the burden on poor districts. In a seminal study of the relationship between district wealth and the education received by students, John Coons, William Clune III, and Stephen Sugarman wrote:

> The consequence of uneven distribution of wealth is wide
> variation in the sacrifice necessary to produce the same
> amount of money. As a result, the multitude of decisions
> that are made by districts regarding commitment to education
> is everywhere weighted by wealth. In order for a poor
> district to procure a school as good as its thrice rich neighbor
> it must be willing to tax three times as hard; even then it may
> well be prevented from doing so by state-mandated tax
> maximums. But in either case it is ordinarily left behind in
> the race for superior schools, for clearly, the rich district can
> always stay ahead if it decides to.[10]

Although economists differ as to who bears the burden of the property tax (the major source of revenue for the schools), many believe that the tax falls most heavily on the poor. In 1955, for example, Richard Musgrave calculated an effective property tax rate of 4.2 percent for people with incomes of less

[9] *John Coons, William Clune III, and Stephen Sugarman,* Private Wealth and Public Education *(Cambridge, Mass.: Harvard University Press, 1970), p. 144.*
[10] *Coons, Clune, and Sugarman, p. 21.*

than $2,000. For people with incomes between $5,000 and $7,500, the effective tax rate was 3.4 percent, while those with incomes of $10,000 and over had an effective rate of 3.2 percent. This study, together with one conducted by George Bishop in 1958, supports the view that the burden of financing the public schools falls more heavily on the poor than on the rich.[11]

If states move to a more equal system of allocating funds for school districts while financing schools through regressive taxes, the battle will be only partially won. The same will be true if states choose to take a passive role. Moreover, even if the courts rule in favor of greater equality of educational opportunity, wealthy families may thwart this ruling by withdrawing their children from the public schools. The latter course of action is unlikely as long as the wealthy can retain control of the school system. For while local control and segregation of students are under strong attack, the golden screen provides a substantial advantage to those from wealthy homes. Of course, the ultimate weapon the wealth warriors possess is the freedom of choice that their money can buy, and they are not likely to relinquish this freedom without a fight.

THE EDUCATIONAL SORT

The public-school system acts as a sorting device that carries high-income, high-IQ students to the top while casually sloughing the "less able" at the bottom. Those who survive the educational sort are either certified for further education or shunted into the labor force or the military. Those unable to survive find unskilled jobs or become unemployed, taking their place at the bottom of the income distribution. Every so often someone from a low-income home makes it to the top and the news media herald the virtues of our "classless" society. Yet day after day the public-school system trains millions of students to take their proper places in the income distribution, and all too often the children of the rich replace their parents in the ranks of the warriors for wealth.

[11] *Cited in James Maxwell,* Financing State and Local Governments *(Washington, D.C.: The Brookings Institution, 1965), p. 131.*

10
WHO GETS THE SHEEPSKIN

*The recondite element in learning is still,
as it has been in all ages, a very attractive
and effective element for the purpose of
impressing or even imposing upon, the
unlearned . . .*
—THORSTEIN VEBLEN

The primary and secondary schools sort students into the appropriate boxes, but their role is minor compared to that played by institutions of higher education. Out of every 100 pupils in the fifth grade in the fall of 1961, for example, 76 graduated from high school in 1969.[1] About 45 of these students entered college in the fall of 1969, and according to the Office of Education only 22 are likely to receive a college degree in the fall of 1973. Of course, some stragglers will enter college later in life, and some may complete their undergraduate degrees in more than four years. Nonetheless, the number receiving degrees will be small. At least for the present, those completing a college education will continue to be members of a favored minority.

TRAINING GROUNDS FOR THE RICH

In the past some colleges and universities have served as training grounds for the rich—playgrounds for those biding their time before taking the reins of wealth and power in society. These institutions have groomed the children of the

---

[1] *Office of Education,* Digest of Educational Statistics *(Washington, D.C.: U.S. Government Printing Office, 1972), p. 8. Hereafter referred to as* Digest.

wealthy to assume leadership roles throughout society by offering both an exposure to education and the appropriate social
graces for a gentleman. As Domhoff points out,

> Twenty-five years ago the importance of an Ivy League
> education could not be overestimated in studying the
> American upper class, and the chances were excellent that an
> Ivy League graduate could be so indexed. From 1900 to
> 1940, Harvard, Yale, Princeton, and several other select
> Eastern colleges brought together the rich from all over the
> country, superseding in importance the local universities . . .
> which had trained members of the upper class of their regions
> for so many generations.[2]

Along with the rise of a national upper class in the late
nineteenth century came the growth of such top-notch board-
ing schools as Groton, St. Paul's, St. Mark's, Choate, Phillips
Exeter, and Phillips Andover. These serve as training schools
where the children of the rich prepare for such elite institutions as Harvard, Yale, and Princeton. Over 130 private schools
cater to the needs of the upper class, and most escape the
attention of the general public.[3]

In a study of one such school—Lawrenceville—Domhoff
found that a remarkable number of the 1965 graduates attended the prestige colleges. For example, 14 students entered
Harvard; 10 went to Princeton; 8 went to Yale; 7 attended
Georgetown and the University of North Carolina; 5 went to
Brown, Cornell, and the University of California at Berkeley;
and 4 attended Bucknell, Columbia, Penn, Stanford, Vander-
bilt, and Wesleyan. Lawrenceville, like other institutions of its
type, filters a high portion of its students to prestigious colleges
and universities.

The role of a limited number of private institutions in train-

---

[2] G. *William Domhoff*, Who Rules America (*Englewood Cliffs, N.J.:
Prentice-Hall, Inc., 1967*), p. 17.

[3] *Typical of the popular view is Christopher Jencks' comment, "A few
rich families use high-cost private schools, but this is exceptional." (See
Christopher Jencks,* Inequality: A Reassessment of the Effect of Family
and Schooling in America *[New York: Basic Books, Inc., 1972], p. 27.)
While it may be exceptional, the role of these schools should not be
minimized.*

ing the rich has been documented by Gene Hawes, E. Digby
Baltzell, and C. Wright Mills. In a study of the New York
Social Register, Hawes learned that Harvard, Yale, and Princeton trained 65 percent of the men who had attended college.
He also found evidence that the importance of these institutions is diminishing with time.[4] In another study Baltzell noted
that five of the eight American Presidents who held office
during the first half of the twentieth century came from
Amherst, Harvard, Princeton, and Yale.[5] And C. Wright Mills'
study of 513 top politicians revealed that over 22 percent
attended Harvard, Princeton, or Yale.[6] These studies suggest
the enormous importance of relatively few colleges in preparing students for leadership roles.

THE RISE OF THE NEW ELITE AND THE
ROLE OF OLD ELITE SCHOOLS

Statistics collected by the Office of Education tell an interesting story about the increase in the number of students attending college. In 1869–1870 resident degree enrollments of
both graduates and undergraduates totaled 52,300, or about
1 percent of the total population aged 18–24. By the 1919–
1920 school year enrollments had risen to 597,900, or about
5 percent of the population. And by the fall of 1968 enrollments had reached 6.7 *million*, or almost *30 percent* of the
population.[7]

As the number of students competing for entry into the
nation's colleges and universities increased, this diluted the
role of the elite schools as exclusive training grounds for
students from wealthy families. For one thing, a large number
of new colleges were established to meet rising demand. More
important, the prestige colleges yielded to demands for a
"balanced" student body and gave more attention in their

---

[4] *Gene R. Hawes, "The Colleges of America's Upper Class,"* Saturday
Review of Literature, 46, 46 (November 16, 1963), 68–71.
[5] *E. Digby Baltzell,* The Protestant Establishment *(New York: Random
House, Inc., 1964), p. 135.*
[6] *C. Wright Mills,* The Power Elite *(New York: Oxford University
Press, 1956), p. 402.*
[7] *Digest, p. 67.*

admissions requirements to the academic potential of students as well as their family background. These policies enabled more students from low- and middle-income homes to gain access to the road to wealth; they seem to have barely affected the role of the old elite schools in preparing their graduates for positions of wealth and power in society.

A remarkable number of graduates from elite schools rise to positions of prominence in society. The civil service does not list its appointees on the basis of their college backgrounds; hence statistics are not available for all federal agencies and departments. It is a simple matter, however, to examine the backgrounds of the members of President Nixon's second cabinet. Elliot L. Richardson (Justice), Caspar W. Weinberger (HEW), and James T. Lynn (HUD) are all Harvard graduates. William P. Rogers (State) is a Cornell man. Thus four out of the 11 cabinet members are graduates of Ivy League schools. If the analysis is extended to include people close to the President, such as Roy L. Ash, a Harvard man now in charge of the Office of Management and Budget, and Henry Kissinger, ex-Harvard professor and the President's chief foreign-affairs adviser, the value of a Harvard affiliation becomes even more apparent.

Harvard graduates appear in cabinet positions with remarkable frequency. Four out of ten members of President Kennedy's cabinet were Harvard men; President Eisenhower's cabinet also included four, and President Theodore Roosevelt's had five (although not all at the same time).[8]

Nor is the government unique in its employment of graduates of prestige colleges. For example, Ivy League graduates hold key positions in the banking industry and in executive positions on Wall Street, at the top of the best legal firms and as members of the judiciary branch, at the head of the nation's largest industries, and as directors of the nation's universities. A casual observer would note a strong relationship between a student's school affiliation and the kind of life he leads later. But does the college a person attends really matter?

[8] *Theodore Sorensen,* Kennedy *(New York: Bantam Books, Inc., 1966), p. 288.*

Does It Really Matter What College One Attends?

The people at the very top of the income distribution need not worry about where their children will go to college or even whether they will go at all. Family assets are sufficiently large so that the offspring of the very rich may never need to work. And should a family member want a job, it would certainly be easy enough for his family to create one.

Why, then, do the children of the very rich go to college? Several factors may be involved. A prestigious college education sets the children of the rich apart from most of the population and helps legitimize their claim to wealth. It also provides exposure to new ideas and different life styles. The college environment contributes to their sophistication and helps shape their view of the world.

For some wealthy students these are the only reasons for going to college; others see the process of education as providing tools that will contribute to their future success. This is especially true of those who wish to pursue careers as top executives, in the professions, or as money managers. Interestingly, however, although Baltzell and his associates find evidence of an upper-class preference for prestigious colleges, few studies have shown that graduates of such colleges *earn more* than other graduates. In a study using 1947 *Time* magazine data, Shane Hunt attempted to determine whether a person's earnings are affected by the college he attends. His results suggest that the institution exerts a small effect on earnings after other factors are taken into account.[9] Other researchers have shown that people of high "ability" (usually measured by aptitude or achievement scores) tend to earn more. Since the prestige schools usually accept high-ability students, the average earnings of their graduates tend to be higher than those of graduates of less prestigious schools. This makes it difficult to isolate the unique effect of a particular institution.

Unfortunately almost no data sources are available that enable researchers to trace the earnings of college alumni over

[9] Shane Hunt, "Income Determinants for College Graduates and the Return to Educational Investment." Unpublished Ph.D. dissertation, Yale University, 1963.

time, possibly because such data are costly to compile and fraught with measurement problems. To account for the effects of schooling, the earnings of college graduates must be measured net of the advantages created by family income, ability, and other individual characteristics. But it is extremely difficult to remove the effects of these items, especially since high-income, high-ability students are usually found at prestige colleges.

Moreover, researchers remain unclear as to how attendance at a prestige school might affect earnings. Perhaps a Harvard graduate obtains a better starting job than a graduate of San Diego State. But if the two are equally competent, they may nonetheless earn an equivalent amount during their lifetimes. On the other hand, if a Harvard graduate, irrespective of his abilities, is promoted to better positions throughout his life, then prestige schooling exerts a long-range effect on earnings. Thus far we do not have a great deal of evidence that attendance at a prestige school makes a difference. Nonetheless, the large number of prestige graduates in important positions lends credence to the view that people who attend these schools make valuable contacts that may be useful later in life.

The Rise of the New Elite

While the very rich have been fighting to maintain their hold over the prestige colleges, those lower down in the warlord group and members of the knight and estate classes have not been idle. Some members of these groups have benefited directly from the liberalization of admissions policies by the prestige colleges. But many have chosen to receive their education at one of a growing number of well-staffed high-quality public universities. Utilizing golden screen admissions policies, some of the "best" state universities limit their admissions to students with "good" grades and high test scores.

WHO PAYS THE PIPER?

Over the years an increasing number of students have entered public colleges and universities. The growth of these institutions has indeed been impressive. In 1950, for example, about 56 percent of the students enrolled at a four-year institution

were attending public facilities. By 1970, this figure had increased to almost 65 percent.[10] Several things account for the
rapid growth of public facilities: (1) Public institutions cost
their students substantially less than private ones, despite
rising tuitions. According to the Office of Education, the
average tuition at a private university during the 1969–1970
academic year was $1,794; the average for the public universi-
ties was $413.[11] (2) In the past 20 years many public univer-
sities have opened branch campuses in urban areas. The
proximity of these schools has attracted many students who
might otherwise not have attended college.[12] (3) Some public
institutions, such as the University of Wisconsin at Madison,
have received sufficient funds to boost substantially the quality
of their faculties. As a result these institutions offer an education on a par with that provided by some of the best private
colleges.

Precisely because public institutions charge low tuitions,
many people believe they provide an equal opportunity to
obtain a "quality" education for all residents of the state. But
this is not always the case. In a controversial study of California higher education, Professors W. L. Hansen and B.
Weisbrod (H&W) found that, although some low-income
students attend the state's institutions of higher education, it
is primarily the students from higher-income homes who go
to the more expensive public universities. Since the state provides a larger subsidy to these institutions, the students who
attend them receive a higher subsidy than those at state and
junior colleges. For example, a student attending the University of California (UC) at Berkeley in 1965 received a
subsidy of $7,140; at a state college he received $5,800, and at
a junior college, $1,440.[13]

A student's eligibility for the UC and other state colleges
rests primarily on his performance in high school and his

[10] *Howard Tuckman,* The Economics of Education *(Joint Council on Economic Education, 1973).*
[11] *Tuckman, p. 3.*
[12] *H. Tuckman and S. Ford,* The Demand for Higher Education: A Florida Case Study *(Lexington, Mass.: Lexington Books, 1972), Chapter 3.*
[13] *W. L. Hansen and B. Weisbrod, "The Distribution of Costs and Direct Benefits of Public Higher Education: The Case of California,"* Journal of Human Resources, 4, 2 (Spring 1969), 178.

achievement test scores. As our earlier discussion suggests, students from high-income homes frequently obtain higher scores on achievement tests. They are also usually able to tap family resources to finance their education. These advantages make it easier for high-income students to attend the UC.

Figure 15 shows the distribution of parental incomes for several different groups. Part I indicates the distribution of parental incomes for families without children in college. Notice that this group has a lower median income than any of the others. Parts II, III, and IV give the distribution of parental incomes for students enrolled in junior and state colleges and in the UC. As we move from Part II to Part IV, it seems clear that people with high incomes prefer the state colleges to the junior colleges and the UC to both alternatives.

The diagram illustrates the types of institutions attended by students from progressively wealthier families. Among students attending junior colleges, those coming from families with incomes of $20,000 or more constitute 6.8 percent. The percentage increases to 7.8 for those attending state colleges and 18.4 for those at the UC. The converse is also true—the percentage of students from homes with incomes under $6,000 decreases as we move from the junior college to the UC. The data confirm the fact that students from upper- and middle-income families represent a large portion of the total attending expensive schools.

It is also useful to ask who pays for the subsidies received by college students. Since public colleges are not financed by a specific tax, it seems reasonable to assume that the necessary funds come from the state treasury. This implies that the colleges are financed by the same tax mix as other government programs. Thus if a state tax structure is regressive (i.e., falls most heavily on the poor), so are the taxes used to provide the public subsidies. H&W find that the *combined* state and local tax structure for California is regressive below $8,000 and roughly proportional (i.e., the same tax rate applies to all incomes) above this level.[14] Thus the poor appear to pay a larger share of the cost of providing public subsidies.

H&W also find that the family of the average college student

[14] *Hansen and Weisbrod, p. 189.*

Figure 15

DISTRIBUTION OF CALIFORNIA FAMILIES
BY INCOME LEVEL AND TYPE OF COLLEGE IN 1964

I. *Distribution of Families Without Children in California Public Higher Education*

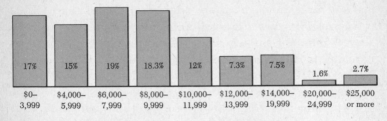

II. *Distribution of Parental Incomes at California Junior Colleges*

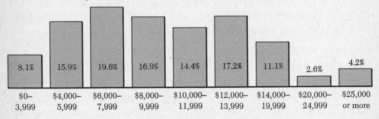

III. *Distribution of Parental Incomes at California State Colleges*

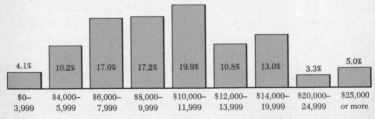

IV. *Distribution of Parental Incomes at University of California*

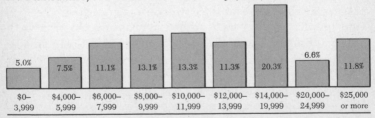

Source: W. L. Hansen and B. Weisbrod, "The Distribution of Costs and Direct Benefits of Public Higher Education: The Case of California," *The Journal of Human Resources*, 4, 2 (Spring 1969), 183.

has a higher income than the average family without children in college. This is shown in line 1 of Table 16. Yet the former pays proportionately less tax (see line 3) and receives a higher subsidy than the latter. The amount of the public subsidy, net of taxes, is greatest at the UC, where family incomes are highest, and least at the junior colleges, where more lower-income families are found. On the basis of these data, H&W conclude that "the current method of financing higher education leads to a sizeable redistribution of income from lower to high income."[15]

These findings cast the role of public colleges in a startling new light by suggesting that the public college system redistributes income from the poor to those with higher incomes. They also provide evidence that the sorting that begins in the elementary and secondary schools continues at universities and

[15] W. L. Hansen and B. Weisbrod, Benefits, Costs and Finance of Public Higher Education *(Chicago: Markham Publishing Co., 1970), p. 77.*

Table 16

AVERAGE SUBSIDIES RECEIVED BY CALIFORNIA FAMILIES, 1964

	Families Without Children in California Public Colleges	Families with Children in California		
		Junior College	State College	UC
1. Average family income	$7,900	$8,800	$10,000	$12,000
2. Average higher-education subsidy per year	0	720	1,400	1,700
3. Average total state and local taxes paid	650	680	770	910
4. Net transfer (line 2 − line 3)	−650	+40	+630	+790

Source: W. L. Hansen and B. Weisbrod, "The Distribution of Costs and Direct Benefits of Public Higher Education: The Case of California," Journal of Human Resources, 4, 2 *(Spring 1969), 166.*

colleges. The H&W data again illustrate the fact that students
have neither equality of access nor equality of opportunity.

Because the H&W study belies the conventional wisdom in
this area, it is not surprising to find it under attack. In a
reexamination of the data, Joseph A. Pechman argues that
H&W are wrong, arriving at this conclusion by a somewhat
different approach. Since H&W are interested in how the
educational system redistributes income by income groups,
Pechman argues that they should construct an income distribution, and he does so. (Contrast this with the H&W method
of comparing the benefits and costs of the subsidy provided to
the *average*-income family at each type of college.) Pechman
redefines the H&W tax figures by adding in the California
corporation tax and the estate and gift taxes. He also distrib-
utes the H&W tax estimates by income class. The resulting
figures are more progressive than those used by H&W.
Pechman then considers the net subsidy (benefits less taxes)
for each income class; his results indicate a positive subsidy to
families with less than $12,000 in income and a negative sub-
sidy (i.e., a tax payment) from those with incomes above
$12,000.[16] He concludes that public education "does about
what its advocates expect."

Pechman's findings suggest that there is no significant redistribution of income from lower- to upper-income groups, and
he castigates H&W for their faulty conclusions. However, he
fails to recognize the importance of the H&W findings. The
H&W study shows that by establishing a set of admissions
policies that discriminate against the poor, the schools ensure
that the major beneficiaries of the public schools will be from
affluent homes. And by financing the public colleges by means
of somewhat regressive taxes, the states ensure that those from
upper-income homes can pay less than they otherwise might
to receive a high-quality education. Of course, among the very
rich (and some families who place great emphasis on the value
of a good education) money is no object and the existence of
subsidized education is irrelevant. But many families believe

[16] *Joseph A. Pechman, "The Distribution Effects of Public Higher Education,"* Journal of Human Resources *(Summer 1970), 361–370.*

that the state subsidy provides a welcome push along the road to riches.

FROM KINDERGARTEN TO THE JOB MARKET

The educational system fulfills the needs of the warriors for wealth very nicely. Children of the very rich are separated from other children at an early age to be sent to elite private schools—part of a world that is different from what most of us know. The education provided at such schools is probably no better than that offered at such outstanding public schools as Bloomfield Hills, Great Neck, and New Trier. But they provide a common bond for the wealthy and perpetuate the customs and mores of the upper classes. And they enable the wealthy to seclude themselves from more common folk.

Children from families that are above the threshold of affluence but below the top of the income distribution usually attend a public school in a wealthy community. Because of the golden screen policies of such schools, these children usually receive the best resources and care that the public schools can offer. And many receive an education, if not a certification, on a par with that given to those attending private schools.

A similar sorting process takes place at the nation's colleges and universities. The effects of this process are apparent when we examine the earnings of people with different levels of education. Those who start in low-income homes are less likely to enter a four-year university and more likely not to finish their schooling than those from upper-income homes. Occasionally an exceptionally bright student makes it through the system, and local school officials cry: "The system works," "Horatio made good," "Ability triumphs." But how many millions fall by the wayside, ignored by those around them? It is clear that from kindergarten to the job market our educational system favors the warriors for wealth.

11
THE SHAPE OF THE FUTURE

The purse of the people is the real seat of sensibility. Let it be drawn upon largely, and they will listen to truths which could not excite them through any other organ.
—THOMAS JEFFERSON

Down through history march the warriors for wealth. Well-financed, well-trained, and highly motivated, these brave warriors shape our economic, political, and social system. Each generation the faces change, and so do the weapons used to fight the war. But the pursuit of wealth links the generations of warriors together in a golden chain that slowly winds its way through time.

What accounts for the recent success of the war for wealth? Perhaps the most important factor has been society's willingness to reward those who achieve high incomes with praise and deference. For millions of Americans the pursuit of wealth is not *a* goal but *the* goal in life. A person receiving a large income has concrete proof of his worth. His five-, six-, or even seven-figure income provides a justification of his existence not only to neighbors and friends but to his wife and children as well.

While many economists shrink from interpersonal comparisons based on income, others have no such compunction. Income is the yardstick by which people measure a person's worth. And wealth is a goal toward which human activity is directed. In a social system of this type, a war for wealth is hardly surprising; its ends, if not its means, are consonant with those of a majority of Americans.

It follows that a program that appeals to the acquisitive instincts of the public is likely to find many supporters. This point is of great value to the beneficiaries of the war for wealth. For example, if the very rich had been the *only* ones to benefit from the capital gains provision, it might have been eliminated long ago. But they are not, and this is no accident. By encouraging others to invest in stocks and other capital assets, the warriors for wealth create a broad-based opposition to proposals for reform. And by capitalizing on people's dreams, they encourage even those with low incomes to think twice about eliminating special treatment of capital gains. The appeal is simple: "Support special capital gains treatment now and when you are wealthy you too can take advantage of the provision." If this argument fails there is always the dire-calamity approach: "Eliminate special treatment of capital gains and investors will no longer be willing to make risky investments. Then where will *you* be?" The approaches may differ, but the appeal is always to people's selfish instincts.

The same may be said for "share the wealth but not very much," or so-called trickle-down theories. The travel-and-expense deduction applies to millions of Americans—yet relatively few can charge a company apartment, a yacht, or the costs of a luxury resort on a tropical island to taxpayers. Public irrigation programs, farm subsidies, and education programs provide something for almost everyone, although not in equal amounts.

Internalization of wealth, the process by which the warriors for wealth capture a large share of the benefits of public programs for themselves, is an accepted part of our daily life. Indeed, in one form or another many people try to gain a portion of public wealth for themselves. The farmer seeks price support, the defense contractor a large contract, the realtor low-cost public land, the exporter a subsidy, and the local radio station owner a license to monopolize. With so many hands held out to the government, few are left to hold back the internalization process. And so the war for wealth continues, largely free of public interference or even public concern.

THE WARRIORS FOR WEALTH

How do the warriors for wealth differ from the people around them? First, they are likely to be (although they need not be) above the threshold of affluence. In Chapter 1 we defined this threshold at $14,589 for a family of four in 1969. Families with incomes above this threshold can live a reasonably comfortable life. Many are in a position to spend at least a portion of their time pursuing wealth rather than simply trying to survive. These are usually the beneficiaries of the "share the wealth but not very much" policies, and it is from their ranks that the warriors for wealth are likely to be drawn.

At first glance families earning $15,000 a year have little in common with the very rich—but first impressions can be deceiving. Although the life styles of the two groups are different, their economic and financial interests often are not. Both tie their fortunes to the operation of the economic system, and even though the very wealthy are relatively free from the daily vicissitudes of life, they, like those with only $15,000 a year in income, ultimately depend on the war for wealth to increase their wealth.

Numerous examples can be found of the identification of interests between people with moderate and high incomes. A loan to Lockheed saves the engineer's hide as well as the banker's; yearly farm subsidies supplement the incomes of farmers as well as those of executives of huge agribusinesses; highway programs provide high wages to skilled construction workers as well as windfall profits to contractors; and so on. An even more direct identification occurs in the case of the lawyer, banker, or stockbroker whose income depends directly on what he can do to further the interests of a rich client. The sons of the very rich may attend Choate while those of the accountant enter Great Neck; the very rich may winter in Gstaad while the $15,000-a-year family vacations in Florida. Although their life styles differ, they need only agree on the policies that are of mutual benefit, especially if by privatizing their wealth the rich can minimize differences. (Recall that privatization refers to the fact that whenever possible the rich now tend to consume privately rather than publicly.)

To be a warrior for wealth, an individual must not only have enough money to be able to pursue wealth but also be engaged in this pursuit. Within this category we may include some accountants, bankers, financiers, advertising men, lawyers, judges, lobbyists, public-relations specialists, small business-men, and corporation executives. Also eligible are a host of investors, speculators, real-estate owners, and other "money men" concerned with internalizing wealth to their own (or their clients') advantage. Of course, not all politicians are warriors for wealth, nor are all lawyers or corporate executives. Nonetheless, some people in these occupations are actively engaged in changing the social and economic system to fit the needs of those with the highest incomes, and while their direct interests are not the same as those of the very rich, they have created a set of institutions and mores that over the genera-tions have been especially favorable to people with high incomes.

Providing a second line of support for the warriors for wealth are millions of people who know little about the war for wealth but who doggedly defend their own special privi-leges. To ignore these people would be to sadly underestimate the support wealth warriors can draw. A farmer receiving a grain subsidy of $4,000 a year is not a disinterested observer when a change in the farm program is proposed; a person who owns a summer cottage or a piece of land in the mountains is unlikely to submit quietly to elimination of the homeowner's interest deduction in the federal tax law or reform of a wide range of other government housing programs. Too many critics of the social and economic system blame the rich and the superrich for the present state of affairs. Yet this is too facile an argument. The blame belongs to all who favor a system of special interests, including those benefiting only indirectly from the war for wealth.

CAN THE GOLDEN CHAIN BE BROKEN?

Without major reforms, not only in our social and economic institutions but also in the thinking patterns of individuals, the golden chain cannot be broken. Acquisitiveness seems to be a basic part of man's nature, and it will not be wished away by social visionaries. Most Americans are strongly wedded to their possessions and way of life; major changes in the property laws or social institutions are likely to be met with fear, if not outright resistance.

Nevertheless, several forces are at work that may place limits on the gains the warriors for wealth can make. First, the share of national income going to property has decreased over time while that received by labor has increased. Since the returns to property are highly concentrated, whereas those to labor are less so, this shift may lead to a more equitable distribution of the nation's output of goods and services. Such a shift need not imply, however, that people with concentrated capital holdings will exercise less control over the economy than they did before. As long as power remains concentrated in the hands of the few, little will change. Nonetheless, the shift in national income distribution leads to a situation in which it is *potentially* easier to reduce the control of the rich, assuming that the public is willing to support policies that limit concentration of wealth.

Also contributing to the containment of the warriors for wealth may be the increasing number of students continuing their education. When the number of college graduates entering the labor force was small, most of these graduates could expect to enter into worthwhile and often important positions in the labor force. These students had neither the time nor the interest to question existing institutions. With the onset of mass higher education, however, college graduates can no longer automatically expect to enter fulfilling positions when they leave school. The jobs some take may underutilize their skills and be, in Paul Goodman's words, "not even unquestionably useful."[1] Torn by self-doubt, left discontented by their position in the labor force, and bored by their work, these students are likely to abandon the pursuit of wealth in favor of jobs with meaning.

In the early 1970s, for example, hundreds of law school

[1] *Paul Goodman*, Growing Up Absurd *(New York: Vintage Books, 1960), p. 18.*

graduates turned their backs on the traditional law firms to become poverty lawyers. And in surveys conducted in 1971 and 1972, many students expressed a desire to forgo a career in business in favor of socially relevant, albeit low-paying, occupations like social welfare. For these students and others like them the pursuit of happiness and the pursuit of wealth are not synonymous. Well-educated, relatively well-informed, and highly idealistic, they are anathema to the warriors for wealth—for as their ranks grow, so will the opposition to the war for wealth.

The war for wealth is also threatened by the increasing flow of information to the populace. Americans are better informed about national news events than ever before. The TV networks, together with mass circulation news magazines and local newspapers, provide fairly up-to-date coverage of the actions of the nation's leading corporations and of Congress. And several high-quality television programs have presented careful studies of government subsidies to the wealthy. Together with the coverage given to the "socialistic" loans paid to Lockheed, the wheat sale to the Soviet Union, and other war-for-wealth activities, this bill of fare offers the average American a far greater awareness of the state of affairs than he had before.

In the author's opinion the vast majority of Americans do not want to see differential treatment given to the rich in return for a meager trickle-down of benefits. Once made fully aware of the facts about the war for wealth, few will be willing to bear its cost. It is easy to gain support for a program on the basis of what a person stands to receive rather than what he must pay. But when the benefits and costs of the war for wealth are tallied, many middle-income families will realize that on balance they end up paying more than they receive. Perhaps then they will begin to act.

A full reckoning of the costs of the war will not be easy. It is hard to say, for example, what the interchange of personnel between government and business has cost the taxpayer or what the real effect of the regulatory agencies has been. And even if all of the cost figures can be identified, there is still the problem of presenting them in a fashion the interested layman can follow. None of these difficulties is insurmountable, however, and as the opposition to the war increases, more public pressure for a full disclosure of the costs will follow.

A note of caution is in order. The flow of information to the public will probably never be completely free. Several recent presidents have made concerted attempts to place limits on what may be broadcast—fortunately, with only a modicum of success. And since the owners of local newspapers and radio stations stand to lose from a completely free flow of news, they may exercise control over what may be broadcast. Moreover, as the rich continue to privatize their wealth it will be easier to hide the effects of the special privileges they receive and more difficult to ferret out the costs of the war.

Sooner or later, however, the rising costs of the war for wealth will lead to widespread cries of reform. When this happens, what can be done to break the golden chain? Let us consider a set of proposals.

A PROGRAM OF REFORM

The economics of the rich are neither sacrosanct nor immutable. If our society chooses to adopt a set of programs different from those that currently exist, the war for wealth can be contained. The following is an 11-point program that, if adopted, could alter the course of the war.

1. Combine the federal estate and gift tax laws, and integrate them with the existing federal income tax.
2. Strengthen the antitrust laws to eliminate the major sources of concentration in the business and financial sectors.
3. End tax shelters.
4. Eliminate all deductions and replace them with tax credits.
5. End special treatment for capital gains.
6. Levy taxes directly on the beneficiaries of government programs.
7. Provide a yearly accounting of all tax and expenditure subsidies, and make these subject to review by the budget director.
8. Place restrictions on the personnel interchange between government and business.

9. Improve existing credit institutions.
10. Enrich the environment of the public schools.
11. Establish a set of incentives designed to encourage public participation in government.

The Estate and Gift Taxes

In Chapter 3 we learned that the federal and state estate and gift taxes capture only 6 percent of the total wealth transferred between generations. These taxes barely affect the amount of wealth handed down from one generation to the next. If limits are to be placed on the power of the wealthy, the estate and gift taxes must be restructured. One way to accomplish this is to combine the two taxes and reduce the annual and lifetime exemptions a person is allowed. This would eliminate the splitting of an estate between the two taxes and thus increase the bite of the progressive tax rates. Alternatively, the two taxes might be combined with the federal income tax so that all gifts and inheritances are reported as part of the recipient's income.

The laws governing trusts will also have to be restricted so that the rich cannot avoid taxation by shifting their assets into trusts. A tax might be levied on property held in trust for more than one generation; the amount of the tax would be related to the size of the trust. This allows people to continue using trusts but reduces the erosion of the tax base.

Strong opposition can be expected even on very mild proposals for reform like those discussed here. A change in the tax laws may affect the consumption-investment choice, the work-leisure tradeoff, and the demand for money. Nonetheless, such effects are palatable if they serve to reduce the accumulation of property—and hence of power.

Strengthen the Antitrust Laws

Accumulation of wealth can also be limited by strengthening the antitrust laws. At present there is a discrepancy between the legal prohibition against monopoly and its de facto acceptance. The law provides severe penalties for companies engaged in direct collusion; it does little, however, to break up the large firms in such industries as steel and autos, in which a pattern of administered pricing prevails. All too often the antitrust laws are used to limit smaller firms seeking to acquire power, while the power already possessed by the giants is ignored. Thus many of the family-owned businesses that grew to positions of power in the early 1900s, such as Great Atlantic & Pacific Tea Co. (A&P), Campbell Soup, Ford Motor, and Gulf Oil, have retained an important measure of control over the nation's economy. Some of their leaders have been, and remain, leaders in the war for wealth.

Large family-owned businesses are not the only source of concentration of wealth in society, however. In recent years the growth of giant conglomerates like International Telephone & Telegraph, Gulf and Western Industries, and Litton Industries has led to new concentrations of wealth and power in the economy. All indications point to the continuation of this trend. Willard T. Grimm, president of the Chicago-based merger consulting firm that bears his name, reported that merger announcements increased 4 percent in 1972 and were likely to rise another 5 percent in 1973.[2] Nor do all these mergers combine unrelated industries. PepsiCo Inc.'s recent successful offer for control of Rheingold Corp., already a giant in the beverage industry, is being attacked by some observers as a sign of further "liberalization" in the interpretation of the antitrust laws.[3]

It will not be easy to strengthen the antitrust laws. The industrial giants have sunk their roots deep in the economic and political system. Moreover, the growth of large multinational corporations creates a set of institutions that function, at least in part, beyond the reach of U.S. laws. Overseas acquisitions by U.S. companies were expected to rise by 20 percent in 1973. And the number of large European companies buying American corporations is on the rise.[4]

If steps are not taken to control the growing concentration of wealth and power in our economy, the climate may become even more favorable to the warriors for wealth. What is needed

[2] Business Week, *No. 2262 (January 13, 1973)*, 19.
[3] Business Week, *No. 2262 (January 13, 1973)*, 19.
[4] Business Week, *No. 2262 (January 13, 1973)*, 19.

is a well-thought-out, well-supported antitrust effort, backed by the President and removed from the pressures of politicians who owe their allegiance to large corporations. But such an arrangement is unlikely to emerge unless the public desires it and makes its wishes known.

Eliminate Tax Shelters

A serious effort must be made to rethink governmental policies favoring such tax shelters as investments in oil and gas exploration, in citrus grove cultivation, and in cattle breeding. Presumably the government has created these shelters as an incentive to attract capital into industries in which the public interest would be served by more investment. In practice, however, plenty of investors have been drawn into deals that are profitable only to the hustlers who put them together. Because of the widespread abuse of tax shelters, the National Association of Securities Dealers has proposed limiting the sale of tax shelters by its members to people in *high* tax brackets! And the oil interests have drawn up an Oil and Gas Investment Act dealing with limited-partnership oil and gas arrangements offered to the public. The Securities and Exchange Commission is also seeking to regulate publicly offered tax shelters.[5] But these efforts have no effect on tax shelter deals made privately, and therefore cannot ensure that tax shelters do not lead to a misallocation of resources.

Moreover, all of these attempts at reform avoid the fundamental question: Why shouldn't tax shelters be eliminated? It is difficult to comprehend how the purchase of a vineyard or the raising of minks and chinchillas is in the national interest. As for the raising of livestock, one consultant has stated: "If it excretes it's probably a tax shelter."[6] It would be extremely difficult to show that the social returns to such investments outweigh their social costs. And it would certainly be difficult to defend them in terms of the national interest.

A meaningful program of reform would eliminate both percentage depletion for oil, gas, and other minerals, and the right

[5] Business Week, *No. 2260 (December 23, 1972),* 98–99.
[6] Business Week, *No. 2260 (December 23, 1972),* 98–99.

to deduct intangible drilling and development costs from income. It would end the use of accelerated depreciation techniques for all types of real estate, and it would tax at ordinary income tax rates any depreciation deductions recovered upon resale. The program would also end capital gains treatment for farm income (including income from the sale of livestock), income from the sale of licenses or inventions, and royalties and other income from the sale of timber, coal, and iron.[7]

Eliminate All Deductions and Replace Them with Tax Credits

Precisely because the federal income tax takes a major chunk of income from *most* Americans, an effort must be made to ensure that it does not offer special advantages to a few. Tax shelters represent one form of special treatment and the current system of deductions another. Because of the progressive nature of the tax system, a deduction of a given amount is worth more to someone with a high income than to someone whose income is lower. We referred earlier to this phenomenon as the mathematics of wealth. Deductions were originally permitted in the tax law because the legislators recognized legitimate differences in ability to pay among individuals. Thus a man with no children is assumed to have greater ability to pay than another who earns the same income and has two additional mouths to feed. An equitable tax system should recognize differences in ability to pay but should not make them worth more to the rich than the poor.

A simple way to eliminate the mathematics of wealth is to substitute a system of tax credits for the existing deductions. Under this approach individuals would calculate their taxable income without taking special circumstances into account. They would then subtract a fixed sum for each allowable special circumstance. To illustrate: Suppose that one person figures his tax liability to be $6,000 while another has a liability of $1,500. Each taxpayer has a wife and two children. Assume that Congress decides to allow a $300 tax credit for the

---

[7] *Joseph Ruskay and Richard Osserman,* Halfway to Tax Reform *(Bloomington: University of Indiana Press, 1970), p. 251.*

taxpayer and each dependent. After the tax credit is taken, the former individual pays $4,800 in taxes while the latter pays $300. Under the tax credit approach the $300 credit remains the same irrespective of a family's income; under the tax deduction method the value of the deduction rises with income. The net effect of switching to a credit is to put some of the bite back in the progressive income tax.

As many credits may be granted as Congress wishes. To ensure the effectiveness of the tax credit, however, existing deductions should be reevaluated and greater care exercised in determining which of these will be allowable as tax credits. We have already indicated the perverse effects of the travel-and-entertainment, homeowner, and interest deductions. The decision as to whether to continue the special treatment given these items should be based on a careful evaluation of their social usefulness. Consideration should also be given to the value of providing direct subsidies rather than using an income tax credit approach. If the federal income tax is left with a large number of credits, this will result in a higher tax rate for the average taxpayer than he might otherwise have to pay and the warriors for wealth will have triumphed once again.

End Special Treatment for Capital Gains

Capital gains represent a major source of revenue to the very rich. We have noted, for example, that out of 73.7 million tax returns filed in 1968 only 7.6 million, or slightly more than 10 percent, reported capital gains. Those with incomes of $100,000 or more received over 22 percent of the total capital gains reported, and returns listing incomes of $1 million or more had an *average* capital gain of over $1.3 million. By any standard it must be obvious that the capital gains provision is highly beneficial to people with high incomes. If capital gains were treated as ordinary income, this would eliminate a major way for the wealthy to avoid the progressive tax rates. It would also substantially increase the revenue of the federal government.

At an absolute minimum Congress should adopt the principle of constructive realization of gains at death. Under this principle a tax would be placed on the appreciated value of a stock whenever the owner of that stock dies. This would prevent some capital gains income from escaping taxation completely.

Strong opposition can be expected to either proposal, especially in light of the huge sums they will cost the wealthy. Opponents are likely to argue that eliminating capital gains will reduce the rate of return on—and therefore the amount of—investment. They will also argue that capital gains are different from ordinary income in that they are nonrecurring. But when the smoke is gone one point will be clear: The elimination of special treatment of capital gains can go a long way toward reducing the accumulation of wealth (and power) by the warriors for wealth. A recent study by two Brookings economists suggests, for example, that the federal tax base could be increased by over $26 billion if the tax laws were revised to include both the full value of realized capital gains and unrealized capital gains on assets transferred by gift or death.[8]

Levy Taxes Directly on Beneficiaries of Government Programs

With the number of federal subsidies increasing over time, the public has a right to ask for a thorough reconsideration of existing subsidies. Many programs could be handled more rationally by levying taxes on the people who benefit directly from them. Economists refer to taxes of this type as user taxes. Why, for example, should the public pay to build dams used primarily to irrigate large company farms in the Southwest? Or why should the Interstate Commerce Commission render a variety of services to transportation industries at a cost to all taxpayers? Although several different administrations have considered the question of user charges, surprisingly little has been done to reevaluate public expenditures from this perspective.

As part of a program designed to increase the use of user

[8] *Joseph A. Pechman and Benjamin Okner, "Individual Income Tax Erosion by Income Classes," Brookings Reprint No. 230 (Washington, D.C.: The Brookings Institution), p. 34.*

charges, it would be necessary to identify the beneficiaries of federal programs. Thus far this has not been done in anything but a cursory manner. If the beneficiaries of each federal program can be identified, the full extent of subsidies to the wealthy can be made public. The author's view is that it should be a matter of national policy to limit such subsidies. While there may be cases in which the wealthy must be paid to perform a service of great value to the nation, such payments ought to be strictly limited and a rational tradeoff made between equity and efficiency goals.

Provide a Yearly Accounting of All Tax and Expenditure Subsidies

In recent years the federal budget format has been revised and improved. Special exhibits now provide the interested reader with information on government expenditures for construction, housing, and education. Information is also available on federal credit programs and employment. Since the tax subsidies referred to earlier are not presented in the budget document, there is no comprehensive statement of all of the subsidies provided by government. (Other government aids of a nonmonetary nature are also not included in the budget document. These involve such items as certain types of federal loan guarantees, statistical services, regulatory services, and so on.

If rational policy tradeoffs are to be made, a new format is needed for the budget document listing the value of *all* subsidies made by the government each year. All subsidies should be made subject to yearly review by the director of the Office of Management and Budget so that tax and implicit subsidies, like expenditures, would be forced to compete for funds in the public marketplace. The director, along with the secretary of the Treasury and the chairman of the Council of Economic Advisors, might then make recommendations regarding which tax concessions ought to be increased, reduced, or eliminated. Each year the public would be apprised of annual giveaways in the pages of the daily newspaper, and the victories and defeats of the warriors for wealth would at last be made a matter of public record, along with the results of the latest horse races and the most recent basketball scores.

Restrict the Personnel Interchange Between Government and Business

It may be true that some government activities are similar to those of private business and thus can benefit from being staffed by ex-business executives, but this does not imply that the existing practice permitting free interchange of personnel is the best one. Substantial conflict-of-interest problems arise— as in the case of Clarence Palmby, assistant secretary of agriculture for international affairs, who left the Department of Agriculture to join the Continental Grain Company just a few months after negotiating a major sale of wheat to the Soviet Union. To avoid such conflicts Congress should take several steps, including (1) restricting the income and other services that people concerned with regulating or dealing with businesses can receive from those businesses, (2) requiring a "cooling off" period from the time a federal employee leaves his job to the time he can enter a business having dealings with his previous employer, and (3) limiting the power of political employees to make decisions affecting the firms from which they have come. In addition, severe public disapproval should be levied against political appointees suspected of having previous dealings with government agencies. By this process some of the more obvious conflicts might be reduced.

Steps might also be taken to provide a more professional approach to staffing the positions in the federal government. For example, greater attention might be paid to appointing city managers, mayors, and other state and local officials to cabinet and subcabinet posts. Other potential candidates might include university professors, officials of charities, and health and education administrators. There is no *a priori* reason for believing that business executives have a monopoly on the talents required of good public administrators. Yet many presidents have acted as if this were the case. By insisting on the appointment of officials who will serve the public interest, the public can go far in improving the social and political system.

Improving Existing Credit Institutions

Credit should not be available for people who lack the personal discipline necessary to use it responsibly. Nonetheless, this does not imply that income ought to be the sole criterion for awarding credit. The federal government should provide a program of loan guarantees for poor families who have shown themselves willing to repay a loan but are nonetheless precluded from receiving credit either because the interest rate is too high or because loan funds are unavailable.

The government should also take steps to limit the interest rates loan sharks and juice racketeers can charge. A stiff program of enforcement would be necessary to ensure compliance with government regulations. And steps might have to be taken to ease credit costs to the lenders. If this recommendation is coupled with the preceding one, however, the demand for high-cost loans will fall and most of the loan sharks' business will come from families and individuals who have proven themselves unable to repay past loan obligations.

To avoid the unequal treatment provided to the wealthy through the interest deduction, it will be necessary to eliminate the tax deduction for interest payments. If special treatment cannot be eliminated entirely, it should be continued in the form of a tax credit rather than a deduction.

Finally, the government should scrutinize its own financing mechanisms to eliminate those that favor the wealthy. Restrictions on the sale of Treasury bills should be eliminated, along with the limitations the Federal Reserve places on the interest paid on savings accounts and other financial instruments held by middle-income families. To limit the war for wealth, the federal government must shift its policies from a direction that favors the wealthy to one that is at least neutral toward the various income groups.

Enrich the Environment of the Public Schools

A great deal has been written about whether students really learn anything at school. Much of this debate has been framed in terms of formal measures such as verbal skills, reading scores, and mathematical ability. But part of this debate is beside the point. If the goal of the schools is to provide a fair chance to succeed for all students, several concrete steps have to be taken. These include the following: (1) Provide a remedial program for students with deficiencies when they enter school. Although there is some question whether existing programs of this type have had much success, this does not mean that all efforts should be abandoned. If they are, those who begin life at a disadvantage will have little chance to succeed. (2) Ensure that the distribution of wealth among schools is not a function of the wealth (or income) of the school district. (3) Place limits on the extent to which a school's best resources can be devoted to students in the college track. (4) Continue the search for an improved measure of intelligence. Even though changes do little to promote greater equality of income, they may nonetheless improve the environment in which children grow to maturity.

More is involved than the proposals presented here, however. If the schools are to be transformed from joyless factories to institutions that enrich all of their students, more experimentation must be encouraged. The endless and tiresome regulations of distant boards of education must be replaced by a greater measure of authority vested in principals and teachers. And more local public high schools must learn to give ordinary students the same preparation for college provided by the private schools.

Incentives for Public Participation in Government

Governmental agencies that defend and perpetuate special interests must be subjected to further scrutiny, and so must special-interest groups and Congress. The activities of the various Ralph Nader groups and of organizations such as Common Cause represent a giant step forward. Nonetheless, this activity is too important to be left to a handful of small organizations lacking permanent financing. Perhaps what we need is a new type of public defender who would review the activities of governmental agencies and make recommendations designed to safeguard the public interest. This job would not be an easy one. After all, some congressmen owe their jobs to special interests, and others can be put under heavy pressure to defend those interests when the need arises. In pursuit of his goals the public defender would have recourse to the mass media and ultimately to the wellspring of public indignation. As the need arises, he might also be given the power to enforce decisions deemed to be in the public interest.

We are living at the dawn of a new era. Never before in history have so many people had the time or the resources to do a good job of governing themselves. The opportunity exists to limit the power of the warriors for wealth. But to do so would require the aid of a greater percentage of the electorate than is currently interested in ensuring a fair distribution of income. Perhaps new incentives are required to enlist the participation of the people. We might, for example, pay citizens to participate in local government activities or to serve on national watchdog committees. Or we might hire them to contribute their opinions on a variety of subjects through an independent agency paid out of tax receipts and responsible only to the taxpayers. No matter what method is chosen, the major goal must be to increase the participation of ordinary citizens in the affairs of their government and to increase their understanding of how our economic and political system functions.

THE SHAPE OF THE FUTURE

The shape of the future is in our hands. We can continue to allow the income distribution to be determined by past holdings of wealth and property; by patterns of birth, marriage, and death; and by the war for wealth—or we can apply a set of policies that will call a cease-fire to the war. The means are at hand if we want to end the war. What we need now is the will to use those means.

INDEX